Wellness:

The Awareness of the
Whole Individual

Karen Lindwall-Bourg, MA, LPC-S, FT
Grace Edoho-ukwa, MA, LPC
& Associates of RHEMA Counseling

Wellness: The Awareness of the Whole Individual
©2015 Karen Lindwall-Bourg, MA, LPC-S, FT, Grace Edoho-ukwa, MA, LPC.
and the Associates of RHEMA Counseling

NOTICE OF RIGHTS
Manufactured in the United States of America. No part of this book may be reproduced, transmitted in any form or by any means—electronic, or mechanical—including photocopying and recording, or by any information storage or retrieval system, except as may be expressly permitted in writing by the publisher or author.

NOTICE OF LIABILITY
The information in this book is distributed on an "as is" basis, for informational purposes only, without warranty. While every precaution has been taken in the production of this book, neither the copyright owner nor the publisher shall have any liability to any person or entity with respect to any liability, loss, or damage caused or alleged to be caused directly or indirectly by the information contained in this book.

Scripture quotations are from The Holy Bible, English Standard Version® (ESV®), copyright © 2001 by Crossway, a publishing ministry of Good News Publishers. Used by permission. All rights reserved.

Scripture quotations taken from the New American Standard Bible®. Copyright © 1960, 1962, 1963, 1968, 1971, 1972, 1973, 1975, 1977, 1995 by The Lockman Foundation. Used by permission.

Scripture taken from the New King James Version®. Copyright © 1982 by Thomas Nelson. Used by permission. All rights reserved.

Scripture quotations marked (NIV) are taken from the Holy Bible, New International Version®, NIV®. Copyright © 1973, 1978, 1984, 2011 by Biblica, Inc.™ Used by permission of Zondervan. All rights reserved worldwide. www.zondervan.com The "NIV" and "New International Version" are trademarks registered in the United States Patent and Trademark Office by Biblica, Inc.™

Scripture quotations marked HCSB are taken from the Holman Christian Standard Bible®, Used by Permission HCSB ©1999, 2000, 2002, 2003, 2009 Holman Bible Publishers. Holman Christian Standard Bible®, Holman CSB®, and HCSB® are federally registered trademarks of Holman Bible Publishers.

Scripture quotations marked (NLT) are taken from the Holy Bible, New Living Translation, copyright ©1996, 2004, 2007, 2013 by Tyndale House Foundation. Used by permission of Tyndale House Publishers, Inc., Carol Stream, Illinois 60188. All rights reserved.

Scripture quotations marked (KJV) are taken from The Authorized (King James) Version. Rights in the Authorized Version in the United Kingdom are vested in the Crown. Reproduced by permission of the Crown's patentee, Cambridge University Press.

Print ISBN: 978-1-937660-85-7

eBook ISBN: 978-1-937660-86-4

PUBLISHED BY:
Heritage Press Publications, LLC
PO Box 561
Collinsville, MS 39325

Cover Design: Christine E. Dupre
Interior Design: Lisa Thomson, BZ Studios

TABLE OF CONTENTS

INTRODUCTION

Twenty-first Century Wellness Beliefs
by Karen Lindwall-Bourg 1

CHAPTER

1. **Clarifying the Seven Dimensions of Wellness**
by Courtenay Blackwell Gueta 15

2. **Honoring God with Physical Wellness:**
My Body for His Glory
by Daniel Stein 23

3. **Honoring God with Emotional Wellness:**
God is a God of Emotions Too
by Julie A. Parton 35

4. **Honoring God with Occupational Wellness:**
Stewards in God's Family Business
by Bill Burns 45

5. **Honoring God with Intellectual Wellness:**
A Path to Creative Solutions
by Rickey Hargrave 57

6. **Honoring God with Environmental Wellness:**
Warning—Toxic Environment!
by Audrey Werner 71

7	**Honoring God with Relational Wellness:** Connectedness Fosters Wholeness by *Grace Edoho-ukwa* 85
8	**Honoring God with Spiritual Wellness:** Growing into Godliness! by *Karen Lindwall-Bourg* 97

WELLNESS ASSESSMENT:

The Awareness of the Whole Individual 109

REFERENCES..119

Wellness: The Awareness of the Whole Individual

INTRODUCTION

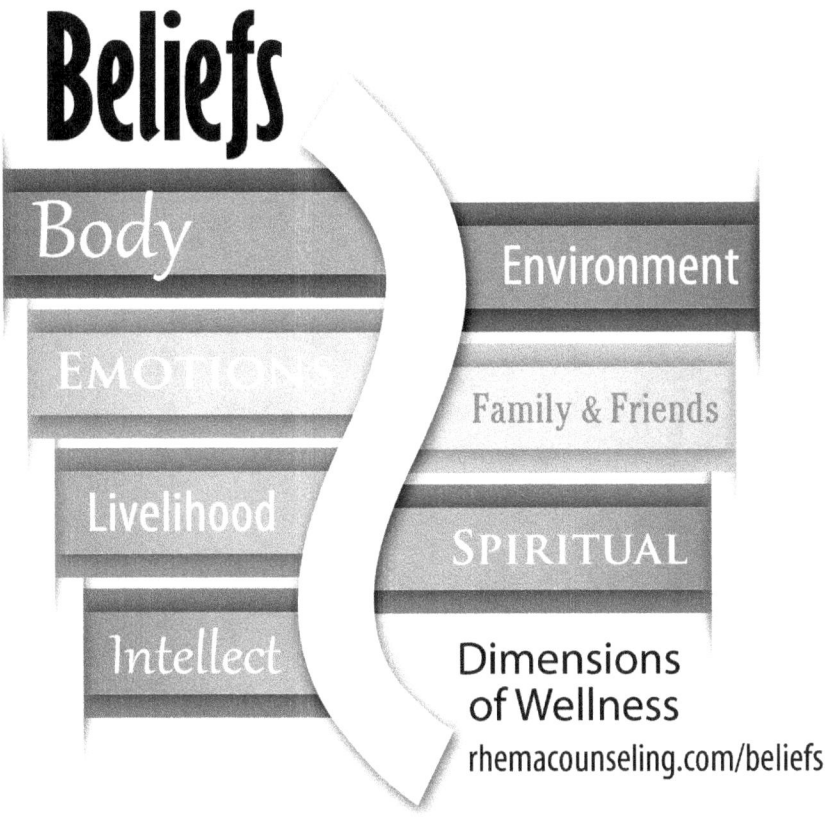

Dimensions of Wellness
rhemacounseling.com/beliefs

Wellness: The Awareness of the Whole Individual

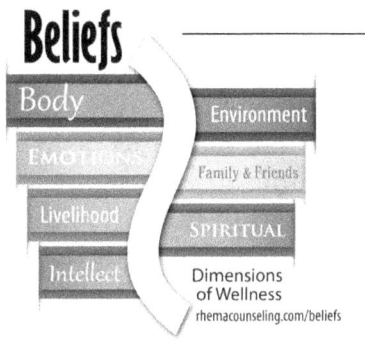

INTRODUCTION
Twenty-first Century Wellness Beliefs

by Karen Lindwall-Bourg

Wellness is an active process of becoming aware of and making choices toward a more successful existence in multiple areas of a person's life.

"Wellness" is the buzzword of the twenty-first century and has been termed "the science of the whole individual."[1] Charles B. Corbin of Arizona State University defines wellness as "a multidimensional state of being describing the existence of positive health in an individual as exemplified by quality of life and a sense of well-being."[2]

The concept of wellness today goes far beyond a single consideration of being physically healthy and knowledgeable about healthcare. In our current culture, there is a growing trend of people looking for a more personalized approach to wellness. People want to be viewed as a "whole person"—they want all caregivers and helping professionals to address other dimensions of their lives. We all want to be well!

Seven Dimensions of Wellness

1. **BODY**—The physical dimension of wellness encompasses commitment to and education about general health and

Wellness: The Awareness of the Whole Individual

strength. It includes regular and safe physical activity, knowledge of food and sound nutrition, and attaining proper and restorative sleep. Healthy families learn to recognize the signs of illness and strive for wisdom when administering and seeking medical care. We are to recognize our bodies as "a temple of the Holy Spirit" bought with a price; therefore, we are to glorify God in our bodies (1 Corinthians 6:19–20, ESV) and care for and maintain our bodies in a way that pleases the Lord.

2. **EMOTION**—Healthy families strive for stable emotions and mental wellness. Families need to be aware of and accepting of individual and collective feelings and enthusiasm for life. Individuals strive to manage their emotions and behaviors within their strengths and weaknesses. They live and work independently while also realizing the importance of seeking and appreciating the support and assistance of others and functioning well within family and community. Mental wellness can be influenced by biological factors, social environments, and family history. We are transformed through the renewal of our minds (Romans 12:1–2, ESV) and the power of the Holy Spirit—the One who produces in us self-control (Galatians 5:23, ESV).

3. **LIVELIHOOD**—We seek occupational fulfillment by choosing a career which is consistent with our personal values, interests, and beliefs, and we work toward financial security. We all want our work (paid or volunteer) to be complete, to contribute to the greater community, to enrich our personal sense of fulfillment, and to contribute unique gifts, skills, and talents toward making life meaningful and rewarding. We strive to be good stewards of what God has given us and meet family financial goals through an understanding of our financial situations and maintaining a balance and comfort with money. We are to work "heartily, as for the Lord" (Colossians 3:23,

ESV) and to use our gifts to serve others and model God's grace (1 Peter 4:10, ESV).

4. **INTELLECT**—Giftedness for learning may vary, but we should all strive to reach our total mental capacity. We are charged to study: "Do your best [study] to present [show] yourself to God as one approved, a worker who has no need to be ashamed, rightly handling the word of truth" (2 Timothy 2:15, ESV). Families want to be creative, stimulating, and growing in knowledge and understanding and potential, seeking wisdom above all. James 1:5 says, "If any of you lacks wisdom, let him ask God, who gives generously to all without reproach, and it will be given him" (ESV). With wisdom, we seek to solve problems, learn through diligent reading and studying, and use creative means to build strengths and talents. Let us model God's grace by serving others through our unique gifts and callings!

5. **ENVIRONMENT**—Families should provide a safe and healthy home and outside lifestyle that honors and respects others and the surrounding environment. They should seek purity and avoid pollution in all entirety. We are charged to care for what God has given us: "The Lord God took the man and put him in the Garden of Eden to work it and keep it" (Genesis 2:15, ESV). And He charges us to provide a home for our loved ones with His wisdom and according to His precepts: "By wisdom a house is built, and by understanding it is established; by knowledge the rooms are filled with all precious and pleasant riches" (Proverbs 24:3–4, ESV).

6. **FAMILY/FRIENDS**—A healthy social dimension of wellness begins with an individual firmly rooted in God's Word, who is part of a unified family seeking harmony and contributing to a whole and supportive community. We strive for good communication and positive interactions, collaboratively seek

Wellness: The Awareness of the Whole Individual

solutions to problems, and support one another during life's trials. "Children, obey your parents in the Lord, for this is right. Honor your father and mother (this is the first commandment with a promise), that it may go well with you and that you may live long in the land. Fathers, do not provoke your children to anger, but bring them up in the discipline and instruction of the Lord" (Ephesians 6:1–4, ESV). This is the charge that brings stability in the family and in individuals' lives as each member is faithful to his obligation and responsibility. Families hold the front lines of responsibility for the welfare and education of their members. What a charge; what a privilege!

You shall love the Lord your God with all your heart and with all your soul and with all your might. And these words that I command you today shall be on your heart. You shall teach them diligently to your children, and shall talk of them when you sit in your house, and when you walk by the way, and when you lie down, and when you rise. You shall bind them as a sign on your hand, and they shall be as frontlets between your eyes. You shall write them on the doorposts of your house and on your gates. —Deuteronomy 6:5–9 (ESV)

7. **SPIRITUAL/SOUL**—Spiritual wellness involves growing in faith and beliefs and seeking meaning and purpose in life. Families strive to live each day in a way that is consistent with their values and beliefs. Spiritually-oriented families appreciate God as Creator and His world around them and learn to value concepts that cannot be completely understood. We strive to know God and His Words (*rhemas*), to meditate and worship regularly, and to share Christ with others. We have hope:

For I know the plans I have for you, declares the Lord, plans for welfare and not for evil, to give you a future and a hope. Then you will call upon Me and come and pray to Me, and I will hear you. You will seek Me and find Me, when you seek Me with all

your heart. I will be found by you, declares the Lord, and I will restore your fortunes and gather you from all the nations and all the places where I have driven you, declares the Lord, and I will bring you back to the place from which I sent you into exile.
—Jeremiah 29:11–14 (ESV)

We seek a full and comprehensive life for ourselves and others: "...I came that they may have life and have it abundantly" (John 10:10, ESV).

SEEKING SHALOM—PEACE

Add to these promising descriptions of wellness: *shalom*, or peace!

HEBREW שׁלוֹם

shalom (šā·lōm)

A common theme for those who seek counseling or help from helping professionals is a desire for peace. Everyone who sits before you is grieving, seeking peace, and/or needing help communicating and moving forward to take steps toward solutions. Their grief may include losses of any kind—they may be experiencing declining or challenging health issues, anxious or depressed emotions and dashed expectations, occupational transitions, intellectual pressures, unhealthy environments, shattered relationships or the death of a loved one, or lack of spiritual peace.

According to Strong's Concordance, there are over 237 Scripture references for the Hebrew word *shalom*[3] in the Bible. Shalom can refer to:

- completeness,
- soundness,

Wellness: The Awareness of the Whole Individual

- welfare, and
- peace!

Consider these uses:

- The word shalom refers to *completeness in number.*
    - The tribe of Judah was wholly carried captive according to Jeremiah 13:19 and Amos 1:6.
    - *We desire to be whole and free.*
- Shalom refers to *safety and soundness and security in body.*
    - Isaiah sought restoration, health, welfare, and deliverance (Isaiah 38:16–17, ESV). Job was promised peace and prosperity in land, cattle, and descendants after his great sufferings (Job 5:23–17, ESV).
    - *We seek restoration and prosperity.*
- In much of the Old Testament, *shalom* refers to *welfare, health, and prosperity.*
    - The Psalmist prayed for peace within (Psalm 122:6–9, ESV). It was common to ask about the times of welfare and prosperity of friends and of enemies.
    - *We desire health and security.*
- *Shalom* is defined as *peace, quiet, tranquility, and contentment.*
    - Isaiah prayed for peaceful habitation, in secure dwellings, and in quiet resting places (Isaiah 32:16–18 ESV). David prayed for the *tranquility of sleep or death* (Psalm 4:9 ESV). Moses was promised contentment and security, direction, endurance, and peace (Exodus 18:23, ESV).

- We pray for quietness and tranquility.
- Some verses refer to *peace in human relationships* (Proverbs 18:24, ESV).
- Other scriptures refer to *being at peace with God*, especially in *covenant relationship* with God (Isaiah 54:10, ESV).
- There is *a peace from war* as communities make peace with one another (Joshua 9:15, ESV) and *during times of peace* (Isaiah 9:5, ESV).
- And finally, peace is used as an adjective. In the Old Testament, God asked for offerings of peace (Deuteronomy 27:7, ESV, and Joshua 8:31, ESV).

So, we strive to be well, find favor, accept friendship, feel great, commit to good health, and seek perfect peace! Remember, *shalom* means peace and well-being!

BELIEFS COUNSELING ASSESSMENT TOOL

At our offices, we love to use the following counseling tool[4] to remind us to attend to all dimensions of wellness when listening to and guiding our clients. We ask them to divide the dimensions into sections and prioritize each one. We give them the fifty-question **BELIEFS** Dimensions of Wellness Assessment (included in the following chapters) to help us assess each area of their lives. They often ask to take a copy home as well.

- **B**ody
- **E**motions
- **L**ivelihood
- **I**ntellect
- **E**nvironment
- **F**amily/Friends
- **S**piritual/Soul

Wellness: The Awareness of the Whole Individual

The Bible talks about being body, soul, and spirit. The following passages from the Bible clearly establish the fact that man is a triune being composed of spirit, soul, and body:

> I pray God your whole *spirit* and *soul* and *body* be preserved blameless unto the coming of our Lord Jesus Christ.
> —1 Thessalonians 5:23 (ESV, emphasis added)

> For the word of God is quick, and powerful, and sharper than any two edged sword, piercing even to the dividing asunder of *soul* and *spirit*, and of the joints and marrow [*body*], and is a discerner of the thoughts and intents of the *heart*.
> —Hebrews 4:12 (ESV, emphasis added)

The *heart* is a fourth dimension!

Even then, there are other dimensions of our lives that fall under these categories—and there are probably as many unique ways of depicting and defining dimensions of wellness as there are individuals!

As individuals and as counselors, we have a tendency to focus on one dimension or the other—whatever is causing us the greatest problem at the time. To assume someone is emotionally depressed without considering physical influences such as exhaustion, thyroid imbalances, or medication influences would be neglectful. To assume someone is safe because they claim they are not being abused would be unwise unless we assess the safety and completeness of their environment as well. We must wisely assess all areas of their lives before recommending various kinds of help.

Even as solution-focused and narrative therapists try to focus on the solution rather than the problem, we might focus on only a few dimensions of wellness to reach solutions. The General Systems theorist proposes that all dimensions are interactive *all* of the time. You are never *not* communicating. You are never *not* relating. And you are never *only* relating in one area or dimension of your life at a time. Remember the song, "The thigh bone's connected to the knee bone…" Everything is connected!

Genogram & Family Map Tools

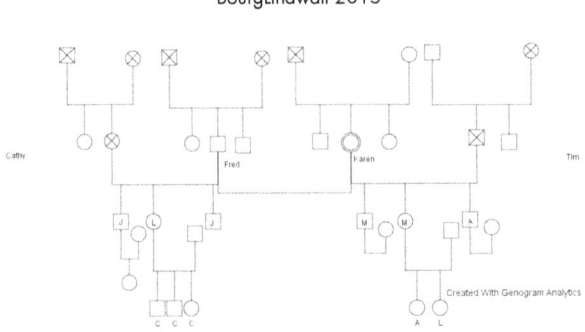

The genogram is a wonderful counseling tool and a beautiful picture of the interactions of many in our lives. So, when my husband, one of our children, and I are in conflict in some way, the tendency is to think of this conflict as one encompassing three people—my husband, our child, and me—when, in fact, this conflict encompasses many relationships:

- my relationship with my husband,
- my husband's relationship with me,
- my relationship with my child,
- my child's relationship with me,
- my husband's relationship with our child,
- our child's relationship with my husband,
- our child's relationship with our parental dyad,
- our dyad's relationship with the child,
- and more…

Wellness: The Awareness of the Whole Individual

Taking this a step further, though, we understand that all six children are affected by this conflict—and so is the grandmother who lives in the house, and so is the dog, and so is the cat. We used our family in our company logo to remind us that we work with all members of a family even when some are not present in a counseling session!

It's important to consider all relationships and assess all dimensions of well-being when working through problems toward solutions at home and in the helping professions. Our doctor, Dr. Timothy Brinkman in McKinney, Texas, is a wonderful physician and extraordinary person. He tries hard to remember and ask after everyone in our large family when we visit. He frequently asks about other dimensions of our lives and has even bent his head in prayer with us during times of great distresses. Those of us in counseling and other helping professions are taught to do a complete interview with clients before we make any recommendations.

We are commanded to listen before we offer wise counsel; we are commanded to accept wise advice and instruction so we may gain wisdom!

Know this, my beloved brothers: let every person be quick to hear, slow to speak, slow to anger..." —James 1:19 (ESV)

Wellness: The Awareness of the Whole Individual

If one gives an answer before he hears, it is his folly and shame. —Proverbs 18:13 (ESV)

Listen to advice and accept instruction, that you may gain wisdom in the future. —Proverbs 19:20 (ESV)

Even in our Christian counseling offices, we might have a tendency to only want to address things from a spiritual viewpoint, but we have an obligation to address all dimensions of our counselees' lives.

Invitation

Join us in the following chapters as we define dimensions of wellness more fully, take you on a journey into each dimension so you can attend more completely to your clients' needs, and share our assessment tools with you!

Send us a testimony of how these tools have helped you and your clients, and we will send you a packet of seven additional counseling tools we love! Please include your name, address, email, and phone number using our form at rhemacounseling.com/contact.

Begin this self-assessment to see which areas of your life need focus and prayer. Each chapter will include more assessment statements for your consideration.

True	False	I attempt to attend to all 7 dimensions of wellness when making important decisions.

Wellness: The Awareness of the Whole Individual

Wellness: The Awareness of the Whole Individual

CHAPTER 1

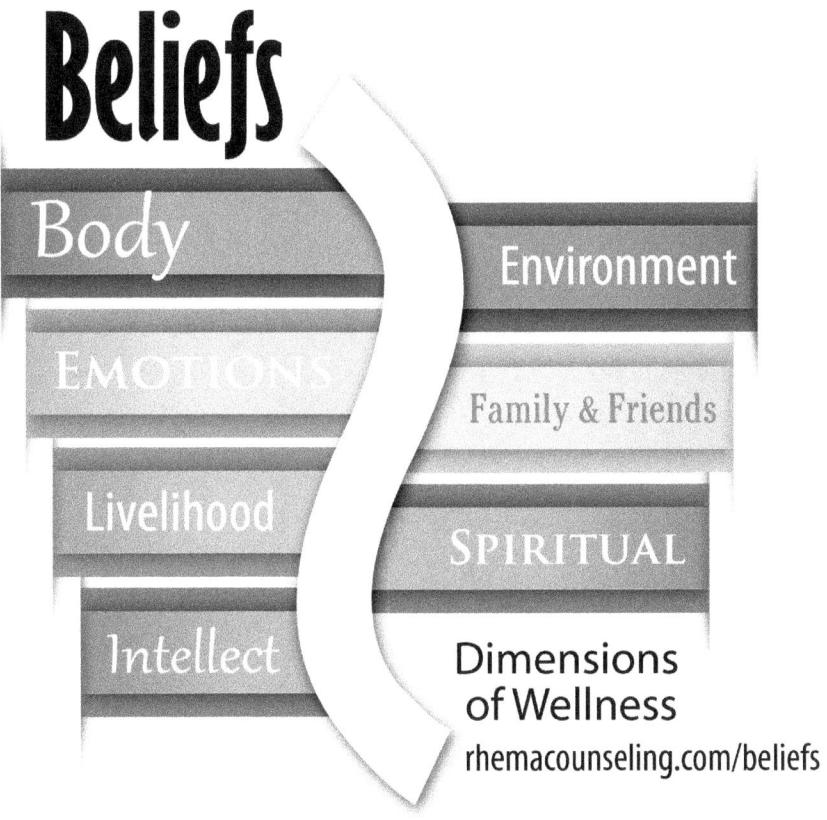

Dimensions of Wellness
rhemacounseling.com/beliefs

Wellness: The Awareness of the Whole Individual

CHAPTER 1

Clarifying the Seven Dimensions of Wellness

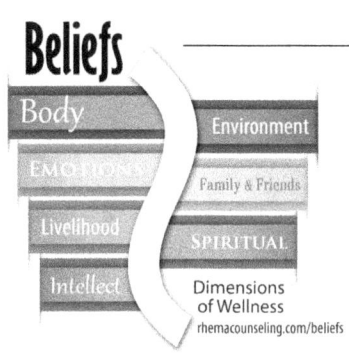

by Courtenay Blackwell Gueta

We are multidimensional beings, and our wellness must be approached in the same manner.

Wellness and health terms are frequently tossed about when speaking of our state of mind and our physical being. Few of us take these terms and consider their meaning and how essential health and wellness are to our entire existence.

Merriam-Webster defines *wellness* simply as "the quality or state of being healthy." *Health* is more clearly defined as:

- the condition of being sound in body, mind, or spirit, especially freedom from physical disease or pain;
- the general condition of the body;
- flourishing condition, well-being;
- a general condition or state.

Because of the importance of wellness and how it impacts our lives, Charles B. Corbin of Arizona State University describes wellness as a "multidimensional state of being describing the existence of positive health in an individual as exemplified by quality of life and a sense of well-being." What does that mean to biblical counselors? How does it apply? Why is it important?

Wellness: The Awareness of the Whole Individual

We will explore the importance of wellness in biblical counseling, its biblical foundations, its definitions, and its applications.

The composition of a human being cannot be reduced to just our physical bodies. We are spirits, with souls, living in bodies (1 Thessalonians 5:23). Our bodies are temples of the Holy Spirit (1 Corinthians 6:19–20). Our *hearts*, also referred to as a further dimension of our souls, are where we invite Jesus Christ to live (Ephesians 3:17). We are multidimensional beings, and our wellness must be approached in the same manner.

We are continually presented with scripture dealing with the spirit, soul, and body. We are warned to guard our heart, for it is the wellspring of life (Proverbs 4:23). The same Spirit that raised Christ from the dead dwells in us (in our spirit) and will quicken our mortal body (physical body) (Romans 8:11).

In order to provide effective treatment, we need to be aware of and address all the dimensions of wellness which impact the spirit, soul, and body. The biblical counselor must consider the following seven dimensions to treat the whole man (spirit, soul, and body).

1. **Body**

    Or do you not know that your body is a temple of the Holy Spirit within you, whom you have from God? You are not your own, for you were bought with a price. So glorify God in your body. —1 Corinthians 6:19–20 (ESV)

    This is all related to the care and maintenance of your physical body. This dimension of wellness concerns exercise and movement, along with nutrition and diet. It also includes health related to sleep and keeping your body physically safe inside and outside your home environment. Regular medical care and responsibility dealing with illness are also part of the physical dimension.

2. **Emotions**

   Be not quick in your spirit to become angry, for anger lodges in the heart of fools. —Ecclesiastes 7:9 (ESV)

   Feelings and emotions are connected to the soul of man, also referred to as the heart. Wellness of emotions for the biblical counselor includes dealing with both negative and positive feelings and emotions. Teaching and counseling clients how to effectively manage emotions is part of comprehensive wellness practice. This dimension also includes addressing an individual's self-awareness, inclination to take responsibility for choices and behaviors, and ability to cope. It explores the role of interdependence of a client in their world.

3. **Livelihood**

   Six days work shall be done, but on the seventh day you shall have a Sabbath of solemn rest, holy to the LORD. —Exodus 35:2 (ESV)

   God wants us to work. The act of productivity is necessary for humans. Work doesn't necessarily have to be vocational or occupational. It can be volunteer or hobby work. Work contributes to the individual's well-being and the well-being of a community. The livelihood dimension also includes financial wellness addressing all aspects of money, including the emotional, spiritual, and physical. Livelihood addresses the balance and health of vocation, occupation, and finance.

4. **Intellect**

   The fear of the LORD is the beginning of wisdom, and the knowledge of the Holy One is understanding. —Proverbs 9:10 (NASB)

Wellness: The Awareness of the Whole Individual

Intellectual wellness is the incorporation of creativity, problem solving, learning, and other mental activities which stimulate and increase knowledge and wisdom. Development and balance in the intellectual dimension aids in the practice of healthy, effective coping skills. Families and individuals can apply creative thinking to problems rather than become stuck in conflict.

5. **Environment**

Let the heavens be glad, and let the earth rejoice; let the sea roar, and all that fills it. —Psalms 96:11 (ESV)

Wellness in the dimension of environment refers to the physical environment. It is the respectful interaction with nature, living things, and the world. Environmental wellness includes taking responsibility for your individual impact on the world. We may also consider our emotional and spiritual environment in an assessment of our wellness.

6. **Family and Friends**

Not forsaking the assembling of ourselves together, as is the manner of some, but exhorting one another, and so much the more as you see the Day approaching. —Hebrews 10:25 (NKJV)

Family and friends are one of the most dynamic of the seven dimensions of wellness. This aspect is not only limited to peace among family and friends but also includes the welfare of the community in which one lives. It encompasses a healthy home, effective communication, and a solid family foundation. This aspect of wellness includes keeping strong relationships, comfortable work environments, including leisure and play.

Wellness: The Awareness of the Whole Individual

7. **Spirit and Soul**

   Now may the God of peace himself sanctify you completely, and may your whole spirit and soul and body be kept blameless at the coming of our Lord Jesus Christ.
   —1 Thessalonians 5:23 (ESV)

   The spirit and soul dimension of wellness deals with one's faith and beliefs. This aspect of wellness is about finding purpose and meaning in life. It is the understanding of something bigger than oneself. It is also the understanding of how one's feelings, emotions, and purpose harmoniously fit into the big picture. The spiritual dimension of wellness seeks to answer, "What is the meaning of life?"

   The part can never be well unless the whole is well. —Plato

   We have to continue to encourage one another to attend to all dimensions of wellness. If we don't, there will be consequences—lapses, imbalances, frustrations, confusions, and incompleteness. If we do there will be benefits—peace and abundant life. There are obviously overlaps in all areas of wholeness. Wellness in one area can improve healthy functioning in all or some of the other areas of our lives.

   Join us as we take you deeper into each dimension, include some special notes about young children, and offer you a free self-assessment tool in the following chapters.

Wellness: The Awareness of the Whole Individual

Wellness: The Awareness of the Whole Individual

CHAPTER 2

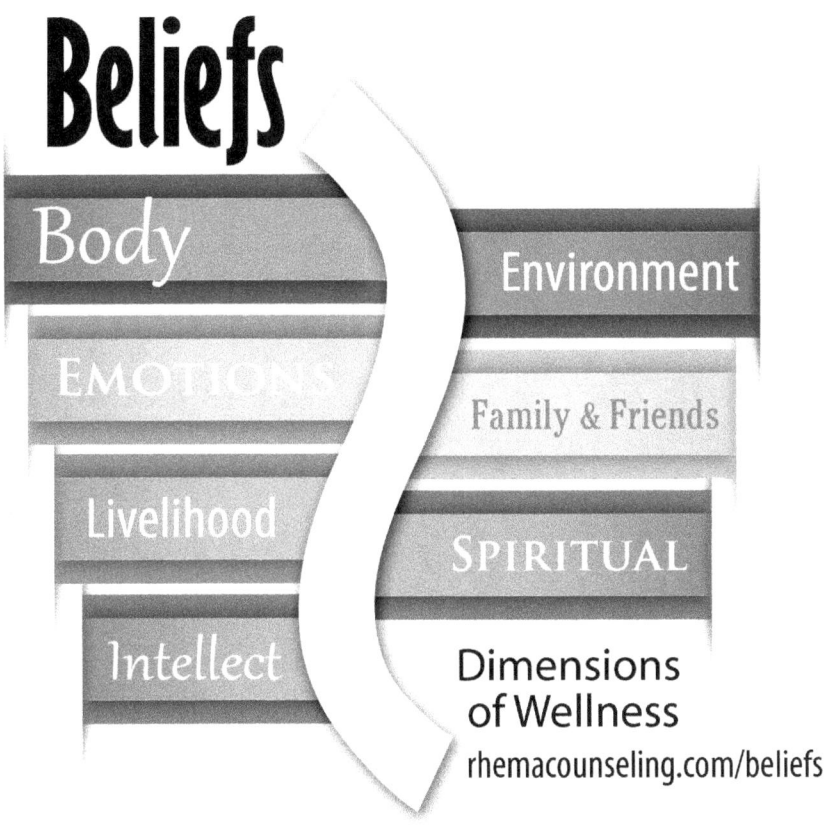

Dimensions of Wellness
rhemacounseling.com/beliefs

Wellness: The Awareness of the Whole Individual

CHAPTER 2

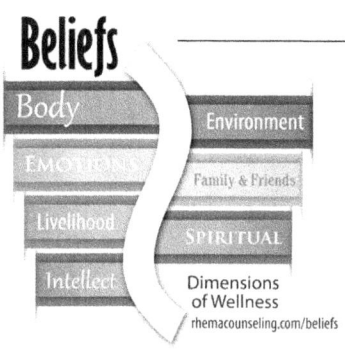

Honoring God with Physical Wellness:

My Body for His Glory

by Daniel Stein

Do you eat and drink food and maintain physical fitness for God's glory?

1 Corinthians 10:31 says, "So whether you eat or drink or whatever you do, do it all for the glory of God" (NIV). Why is it that, as Christians, we sometimes address all the areas of our lives *except* our health? When was the last time you heard a sermon preached on living out a healthy lifestyle? You probably haven't because it is not a frequent focus in the body of Christ. Obesity and health have both been ignored in the church—maybe because this is so prevalent in this culture, it has just become the "norm." But clearly, from this verse (and many others), God is saying that He wants everything that we do to bring Him glory—even what we are putting into our stomachs and how we steward our bodies. Our health and what we eat is very important to God.

Our Mindset Challenges

There are many reasons why we choose not to exercise or steward our bodies the way we should. First of all, we fail to live in the truth that our bodies do not belong to us. 1 Corinthians

Wellness: The Awareness of the Whole Individual

6:19 says, "Or do you not know that your body is a temple of the within you, whom you have from God? *You are not your own,* for you were bought with a price. So glorify God in your body." (ESV, emphasis added). Do you eat and drink food and maintain physical fitness for God's glory?

1 Corinthians 10:31 says, "So whether you eat or drink or whatever you do, do it all for the glory of God" (NIV). Why is it that, as Christians, we sometimes address all the areas of our lives *except* our health? When was the last time you heard a sermon preached on living out a healthy lifestyle? You probably haven't because it is not a frequent focus in the body of Christ. Obesity and health have both been ignored in the church—maybe because this is so prevalent in this culture, it has just become the "norm." But clearly, from this verse (and many others), God is saying that He wants everything that we do to bring Him glory—even what we are putting into our stomachs and how we steward our bodies. Our health and what we eat is very important to God.

Our Mindset Challenges

Our bodies were literally purchased by Jesus on the cross, so we do not own our bodies. They are simply on loan to us, and we are to use our bodies while temporarily on this earth to bring God glory.

For example, if a neighbor asks us to babysit his pet and we agree, we are going to make sure that pet is fed and taken care of every single day. On the other hand, when we have our own pet, we are more likely to become lax with the pet and maybe skip a few days of taking the pet on a walk. I believe if we start with the mindset that our bodies do not belong to us and that we are simply stewards, freedom begins. When something does not belong to us, we take better care of it and have more respect for it.

Wellness: The Awareness of the Whole Individual

Even when we begin to adopt a mindset that "our bodies do not belong to ourselves," we are still faced with many challenges. The biggest challenge (or battle) is in the mind. We have great intentions of stewarding our bodies for God's glory, but we just cannot seem to follow through. Why? We don't renew our minds, and we think our willpower is stronger than God's power.

We also have an enemy. John 10:10 says, "The thief comes only to *steal and kill and destroy*. I came that they may have life and have it abundantly" (ESV, emphasis added). The enemy wants to take our life away from us. He does so in many ways, including by sabotaging our health with diseases, most of which are preventable through a healthy lifestyle. With all these forces working against us, we are in a constant battle to succeed in stewarding our health and bodies for God's glory.

Renewing Our Minds

Change happens under one condition: we renew our minds. Romans 12:2 says, "Do not be conformed to this world, but be transformed by the *renewal of your mind*, that by testing you may discern what is the will of God, what is good and acceptable and perfect" (ESV, emphasis added). Every single day, we either choose to renew our minds with old thought patterns and beliefs (which are often lies), or we renew our minds with truth (the Word of God.) When we choose not to renew our minds, strongholds develop. Strongholds are simply ways of thinking that do not line up with scripture and keep us in bondage.

An example that I see with a lot of my fitness clients would be yo-yo dieting. A yo-yo diet lifestyle is rooted in a stronghold. The stronghold may be different for everyone, but as a whole, it is rooted in self-reliance. A stronghold of self-reliance says, "Today is Monday. I'm going to find a new diet and give it my best this

Wellness: The Awareness of the Whole Individual

week. This time is going to be different." How does that line of thinking bring glory to God? Where in that way of thinking are we asking God for His supernatural help and grace? Clearly, we need God's help; otherwise, we wouldn't need a diet in the first place!

When we *do* reach out for God's help and start to renew our mind, there is an enemy who immediately tries to attack us with lies and old belief systems. The enemy is waiting for us with temptations to go back into our old ways of thinking and living. That is another reason why we must renew our minds. In the process of renewing our minds through the word of God, we can learn how to maintain our victory that we already have in Christ against the enemy.

Daniel's Story

As a certified personal trainer and worker in the fitness industry for over ten years, I have personally experienced all of the above challenges and still face challenges to this day. I am still overcoming obstacles, and there are still days when I let the enemy get the best of me—normally because I become lax in my quiet time and fail to meditate on truth. However, I can say that those occurrences have become fewer and fewer over the years!

I would like to share a little bit about my own personal struggles that I have had with these challenges and how I have used biblical principles to overcome them.

My challenges and bad habits with health and fitness began as early as middle school. As a middle school student, I remember waiting for the bus to pull up to my corner as I sipped on my Dr. Pepper—I never went to school without it. No matter the cost, I always had one ready to drink. When I got to school, my cravings for sugar were only multiplied when I went through the cafeteria line. If my parents didn't pack me a meal, I would go through the lunch line and get a honey bun with multiple servings of fried processed lunch foods. I would even wait until everyone had gone through the line and try and get free extra food! After I ate my processed meal, I would go to the school candy store and purchase my favorite candy—sour straws. If I didn't have the extra money, I would ask my friends for fifty cents. If they wouldn't give me the money, I would actually steal candy when the attendants weren't looking. I guess you could say I had an addiction.

As I got into high school, my addiction got worse. I started working out and playing football as a freshman, but I continued eating processed food and candy and added in drugs and alcohol. I tried my first cigarette and chewing tobacco as a freshman in high school and got drunk for the first time that same year. Now, I was eating processed foods, drinking alcohol, and using chewing tobacco. My food addiction didn't get me in trouble with the law, but my drug addiction did. I received several tickets such as "minor in possession of tobacco" and "minor in consumption of alcohol." Of course, none of that stopped me. I wanted what I wanted and was willing to do anything to get it. I had a serious addiction that started with a craving for sugar and processed food that escalated to drugs.

During my next years of high school, I continued to experiment with different recreational drugs. I was abusing my body and neglecting my health in every way possible. During my senior year, I had a six-hour glucose tolerance test and found out that I was pre-diabetic and had elevated liver enzymes. I was later checked out of high school and into an in-patient drug rehab program. After completing the drug rehab program during my senior year of high school, I started to work out and do weightlifting. I found that weight-lifting was a great alternative to using drugs and alcohol, so those activities become my new "high."

Wellness: The Awareness of the Whole Individual

After high school, I continued my sobriety with drugs and alcohol. I started exercising twice a day—once at 5:00 a.m. and once at 6:00 p.m. I then got into bodybuilding and started using anabolic steroids and fat burners to speed up my results. Since I really enjoyed bodybuilding, I had a good reason to change my diet and stop drinking. I started eating very lean proteins and a lot of complex carbohydrates. I began reading books on bodybuilding and learning about nutrition. My world and life revolved around it.

I had this desire to have the perfect body—like I saw in bodybuilding magazines and on the internet. This desire for perfection led me to develop an eating disorder where I would binge and purge my food. There were times when I would have these uncontrollable desires and cravings for unhealthy food, so I would go on high caloric binges and immediately throw up my food after satisfying my craving. Then, one day in in 2009, everything changed.

While going into the gym for another workout, I crossed paths with a man named Jason. He met me in the locker room and asked me if I wanted to work out with him. I had never seen or met him before, so I was a little disturbed that he wanted to work out with me. He was in great shape, though, so I figured I could learn a thing or two from him. I agreed.

While we were working out, Jason started asking me questions and building a relationship with me. After the workout, he invited me to his church. I was open-minded and went to his church the following Sunday. After a few weeks of attending his church, I realized that I was not saved. In spite of all my drug issues as a teenager, I was actually raised Christian and went to church, so I had believed I was saved. But after hearing several messages from this church, I knew I was not. There was no fruit in my life that would show I was saved, and I had no relationship with God unless I was in trouble with the law and then called on God for help. That is when I gave my life to Jesus Christ, and everything about my life changed.

A Life of Surrender

After I became a Christian, I continued working out and still aspired to be a bodybuilder. However, in my sanctification process as a Christian, I started to be convicted about my motivations for working out. Through the lens of scripture, I realized that the main reason I was working out and eating healthy was not to be healthy and a good steward of my body—it was to gain acceptance and attention from others. I surely did not accept myself for who I was—I was creating an image for myself that offered false security, protection, and identity.

In 2012, I started to experience some back pain. I went to a rheumatologist who diagnosed me with ankylosing spondylitis. With this diagnosis, I was told that I shouldn't do any heavy weightlifting and should focus instead on alternating high, then low-impact repetitions. I just could not accept that and was determined to learn everything about this disease and how it would affect my workout routine. One day, I prayed about becoming a certified personal trainer, and within days, God answered me by sending a personal trainer magazine to my apartment that was addressed to someone else but went to our mailbox. I knew in my heart it was confirmation from God that He supported me becoming a personal trainer. That year, I became certified through the National Federation of Professional Trainers (NFPT) as a personal trainer.

I continued growing as a new Christian and learning about personal training. I had a full-time job in banking and started to train clients on the side part-time. As I grew as a Christian, I couldn't help but see health and fitness through the lens of scripture. I saw so many scriptures that related to health and was convicted about how I took care of my body. I was eating well and had a six-pack and huge arms, but I still felt unhealthy.

Value Godliness Above All

On the other hand, discipline yourself for the purpose of godliness; for bodily discipline is only of little profit, but godliness is profitable for all things, since it holds promise for the present life and also for the life to come. It is a trustworthy statement deserving full acceptance....(1 Timothy 4:7-9 ESV)

The Lord pointed out to me that although the body is of some value, godliness is to be valued above all things. My entire fitness journey was about idolatry—making an image for myself that ultimately took the place of God. Even as a growing Christian, I would still make my health and fitness more important than my relationship with God. If it came down to missing a workout or missing time reading scripture, I would surely choose to miss my reading time.

As I matured as a Christian, I started realizing the importance of putting God first in my life—before my workouts and before anything else. As I began that process, God laid on my heart a desire to start a biblically based personal training business called Metanoia Fitness. *Metanoia* comes from the word *repentance*, which means "to change the way you think." I wanted to have a different approach to fitness—one that would help people draw closer to the heart of God rather than making idols of their bodies, something I had done for so many years. I knew the only way I could glorify God through health and fitness was if I made physical fitness and health about *Him* and not me.

Through the process of starting my own business and becoming certified, I am still learning to honor God with health and fitness.

As a business owner, my heart desire is to teach my clients the same thing—how to honor God through health and fitness.

Honoring God with Our Bodies

Although there are many ways we can honor God with our bodies, one of the most impactful ways I have learned to honor God with health and fitness is through renewing my mind and meditating on scripture. This process can take place both inside and outside of the gym, but it primarily occurs in a quiet, secret space before God. Jesus Himself often withdrew to secret places. Luke 5:16 says, "But he would withdraw to desolate places and pray" (ESV).

I've found that in this quiet, secret place, my motivations for working out change. My thoughts about working out change from, "I have to have the perfect body," to asking, "God, how can I glorify You with my body today?" My desire and cravings for bad food change. It is in this quiet place that I can ask God for His help to change my taste buds for the right foods that are good for my body. It is in this haven that I can ask Him to make me captive to His desires and to His glory when I work out—not to my own. It is in this space that I can ask Him to give me more energy through health and fitness so I can be a better lover of people and of God.

Try this self-assessment to see which areas of your life need renewed focus and prayer:

Wellness: The Awareness of the Whole Individual

True	False	I honor God by paying attention to and caring for my physical health.
True	False	I treat my body as a temple of the Holy Spirit that is on loan to me.
True	False	My body belongs to God.
True	False	I exercise at least three times a week.
True	False	I am consciously aware of what I am eating and drinking and what is good for my body.
True	False	When I go grocery shopping, I normally look for nutritious items.
True	False	I want to learn how to honor God in this area of my life.
Total ____	Total ____	

Wellness: The Awareness of the Whole Individual

CHAPTER 3

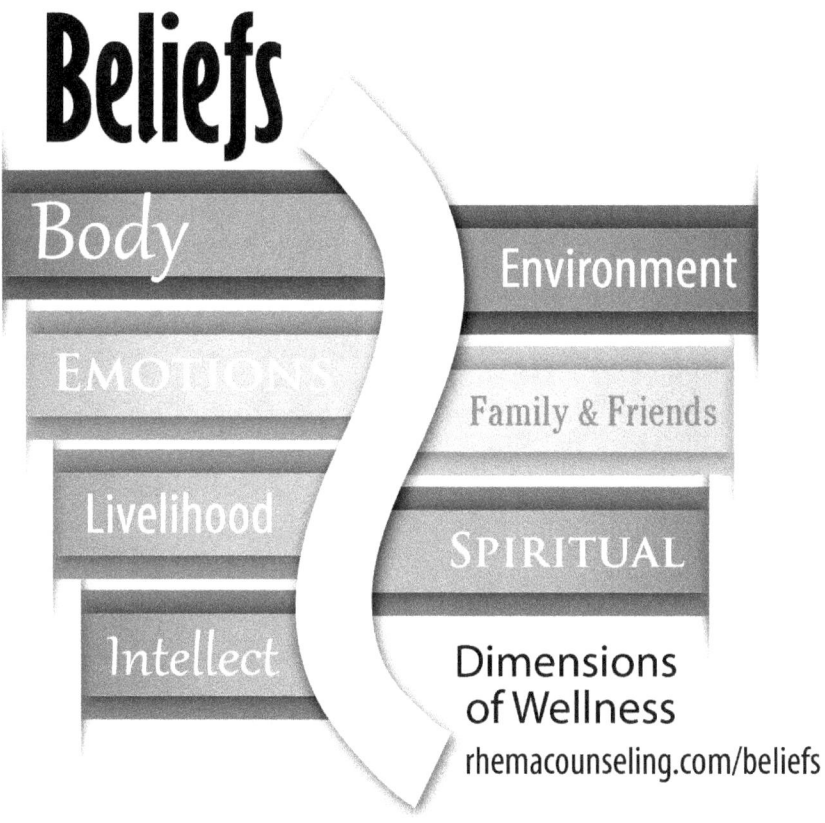

Dimensions of Wellness
rhemacounseling.com/beliefs

CHAPTER 3

Honoring God with Emotional Wellness:

God is a God of Emotions Too

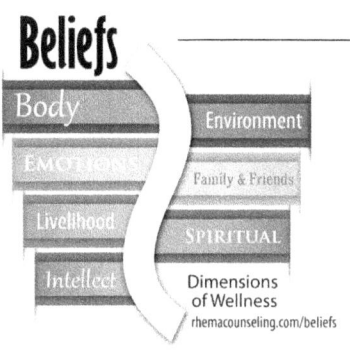

by Julie A. Parton

The better we know Him and thereby allow His Holy Spirit to control our thinking and decision-making, the more our emotions will reflect Him though His image in us.

The most interesting thing about well-being or wholeness concerning our emotions is probably that when we are experiencing emotion, we are often completely *unaware* of it.

Isaiah 26:3 says, "You will keep in perfect peace those whose minds are steadfast, because they trust in You. (NIV)" Or, as *The Message* states it, "People with their minds set on You, You keep completely whole, steady on their feet . . ."

Perfect peace—steady, calm, and confident in who we are and who the Lord is. That is the emotional state in which we would all like to live. But if we were to find ourselves at such a point, do we think we could recognize it? Chances are we would be so focused on serving others and hearing the Lord's direction for ministry to *them* that we would not be thinking about *ourselves* at all.

It is when our emotions are up and down and all over the place that we are most cognizant of them—and so are the people around us!

Wellness: The Awareness of the Whole Individual

"Wow, he is really grumpy today."

"I do not want to be around when *she* gets mad!"

"She is so busy jumping for joy that she cannot get anything done!"

Why Do We Have Emotions?

Why do we have emotions, anyway? Where do these feelings originate? They are part of being made in the image of God. God has emotions; He feels things. We certainly see emotions in the incarnate Christ. Jesus wept with sadness at the death of His friend Lazarus (John 11:35). He was angry with the money-changers and merchants when He cleansed the Temple twice, both at the beginning of His ministry (John 2) and again toward the end of it (Matthew 21).

The Old Testament (especially the Minor Prophets) often refers to God's sadness at the unfaithfulness of His people—their idolatry and seeking after the world's gods:

> When Israel *was* a youth I loved him,
> And out of Egypt I called My son.
> The more they called them,
> The more they went from them;
> They kept sacrificing to the Baals
> And burning incense to idols.
> Yet it is I who taught Ephraim to walk,
> I took them in My arms;
> But they did not know that I healed them.
> I led them with cords of a man, with bonds of love,
> And I became to them as one who lifts the yoke from their jaws;
> And I bent down *and* fed them.
> —Hosea 11:1–4 (NASB)

Wellness: The Awareness of the Whole Individual

Psalm 103 clearly describes the emotions of a person when it says:

The Lord is compassionate and gracious,
Slow to anger and abounding in loving-kindness.
He will not always strive *with us*,
Nor will He keep *His anger* forever.
He has not dealt with us according to our sins,
Nor rewarded us according to our iniquities.
For as high as the heavens are above the earth,
So great is His loving-kindness toward those who fear Him.
—Psalm 103:8–11 (NASB)

Godly Emotions

So, these feelings or emotions we have as humans come from our Maker, the One in Whose image we are created. But there is one huge difference: not *all* of God's attributes are replicated in His created human beings—things like His immutability, His omniscience, His sovereignty, or His omnipotence. Some of those qualities are what permit Him to keep the previously-mentioned emotions in perfect balance—to only be *righteously* angry or sad or disappointed.

We don't have access to that same set of checks and balances. So, how are we supposed to control our emotions so they are a positive aspect of our well-being and don't destroy it? 1 Thessalonians 5:23 tells us, "Now may the God of peace Himself sanctify you entirely; and may your *spirit* and *soul* and *body* be preserved complete, without blame at the coming of our Lord Jesus Christ" (NASB, emphasis added).

The Triune Human Being

That passage teaches us that there are three components that comprise human beings—spirit, soul, and body. The body is

Wellness: The Awareness of the Whole Individual

obviously the physical element, the spirit is the part that relates to God, and the soul is the personality, including the emotions. Paul, the author of 1 Thessalonians, is praying that *all* aspects of the person will be sanctified (or made increasingly like Jesus Christ) and that *all three* components will be preserved in a whole and blameless state. How?

We know that the Holy Spirit interacts with our spirit (Romans 8) to "train" it to live as the Lord directs, making God-directed choices that result in spiritual growth. 1 Corinthians 15 teaches us that there will be a bodily resurrection that will someday perfect these imperfect shells in which we reside. That takes care of two out of three! But what about the soul and those "soulish" feelings or emotions? Who or what is shaping, molding, and maturing those?

Transforming Our Thinking

How do we reach the point of being calm, confident, and so "un-emotional" that we can experience the perfect peace that serenely reflects God's presence and control in our lives?

I would submit that we control and direct our emotions by controlling and directing our *thinking*. Proverbs 23:7 says, "For as he thinks within himself, so he is" (NASB). And in Romans 12 where we are instructed to not be conformed to the world, the opposite of that conforming is stated as being "transformed by *the renewing of your mind*, that you may prove what the will of God is, that which is good and acceptable and perfect" (NASB, emphasis added).

We are not told to change or transform our feelings but, instead, our thinking. What we think determines how we feel (and, consequentially, how we behave.) Consider two people in the same family, for example, who are both dealing with the same tragic event that has just transpired—say, the death of their mother. One of them is weeping uncontrollably, bemoaning her loss, and wondering aloud how God could be so cruel as to take her mother at her relatively-young age of 65. The other sibling is calm, soothing, responding gently and compassionately to all those around, and even comforting the caregivers.

Responses

"Aren't you upset that Mom died?" the first sibling sobs.

The second replies, "Of course I'm sad she's gone, and I'll miss her terribly. But we all diligently prayed that God would be merciful and take her quickly instead of allowing her ALS to continue to deteriorate her body beyond all comprehension. He mercifully answered that prayer that she and all of us prayed. So, am I supposed to be sad or upset that He answered our prayers? He did what we asked, gave us what we begged for. I am grateful."

What influenced the different responses of these two who were dealing with the same loss? Their thinking. The way they viewed the situation. Their perspective. Two different perspectives on the same situation result in two totally different sets of emotions.

Positive Self-Talk

Have you ever found yourself responding inappropriately or in an immature way to a situation in your life? Sometimes, when I recognize what I'm doing, I say to myself, "You need to talk yourself through this." So, I begin to examine my self-talk (everybody has it, whether you like the term or not). What am I telling myself? How do I know it's accurate? Would an objective observer look at the situation the same way? Is there another way to view this? What would it sound or look like? Which honors the Lord more? Does the Bible have anything to say on this topic?

Wellness: The Awareness of the Whole Individual

Usually, once I begin to examine my thinking along these lines, I can identify the fallacies—or at least the shortcomings—in my thinking and bring my perspective more in line with one that honors the Lord and mellows out my over-the-top response at the same time.

Rejoice! Transformed Emotions

Although I've mainly discussed *negative* emotions, feelings that we would like to limit or eliminate from our lives—anger, sadness, anxiety, worry, resentment, jealousy—there are also *positive* emotions: joy, gratitude, happiness, relief, and so on.

Philippians 4:4 commands, "Rejoice in the Lord always; again I will say, rejoice!" (NASB). So, the feeling and expression of joy are something the Lord wants to see in us. Why? Because as the passage goes on to state, that rejoicing is a manifestation of *appropriate and transformed thinking*:

> Be anxious for nothing, but in everything by prayer and supplication with thanksgiving let your requests be made known to God. And the peace of God, which surpasses all comprehension, will guard your hearts and your minds in Christ Jesus. Finally, brethren, whatever is true, whatever is honorable, whatever is right, whatever is pure, whatever is lovely, whatever is of good repute, if there is any excellence and if anything worthy of praise, let your *mind* dwell on these things. —Philippians 4:6–8 (NASB, emphasis added)

Once more, it all comes back to correct thinking producing correct, appropriate, God-honoring feelings and emotions. And the combination of that thinking and those feelings results in *peace*, right back where this chapter started.

No God? *No* peace. *Know* God, *know* peace.

Wellness: The Awareness of the Whole Individual

The better we know Him and thereby allow His Holy Spirit to control our thinking and decision-making, the more our emotions will reflect Him though His image in us.

Try this self-assessment to see which areas of your life need renewed focus and prayer:

True	False	
True	False	I desire perfect peace – to be steady, calm, and confident in who I am and Who the Lord is.
True	False	Emotions are natural – a part of being made in the image of God.
True	False	The Holy Spirit will interact with my spirit to train me to live as the Lord directs.
True	False	To direct my emotions, I have to direct my thinking according to God's will.
True	False	I strive to bring my perspectives in line with those that honor God.
True	False	I desire to Rejoice in the Lord always!
True	False	I want to learn how to honor God in this area of my life.
Total ___	Total ___	

Wellness: The Awareness of the Whole Individual

Wellness: The Awareness of the Whole Individual

CHAPTER 4

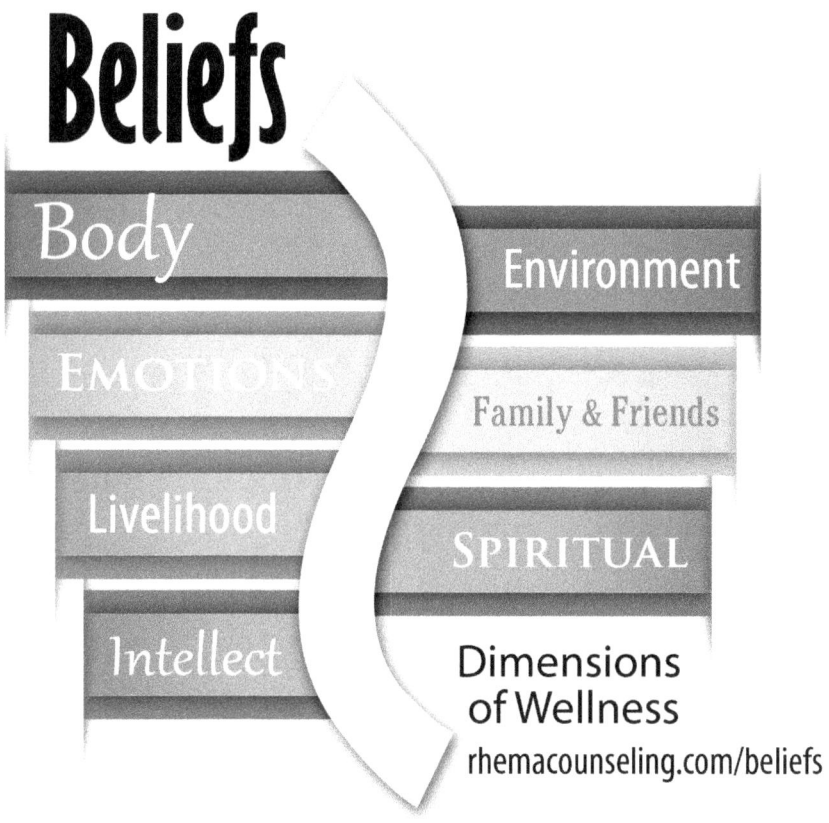

Dimensions of Wellness
rhemacounseling.com/beliefs

Wellness: The Awareness of the Whole Individual

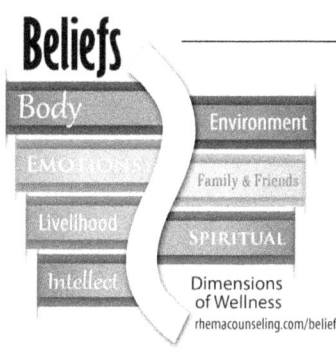

CHAPTER 4

Honoring God with Occupational Wellness:

Stewards in God's Family Business

by Bill Burns

Then I considered all that my hands had done and the toil I had expended in doing it, and behold, all was vanity and a striving after wind, and there was nothing to be gained under the sun.
—Ecclesiastes 2:11 (ESV)

"Work" is a funny word. It can have positive connotations, as in, "That works for me!" But it often has negative connotations for us. "All work and no play" does not lead us to a sense of wellness. The writer of Ecclesiastes recognized that, just like every other pursuit "under the sun," work in and of itself does not produce ultimate satisfaction. So, how are we to think about our lives at work? Whether you are an engineer, a stay-at-home parent, a student, a factory worker, or a cashier, all of us spend more of our lives engaged in some kind of work than we do in anything else except sleep. How can our livelihoods contribute to our wellness rather than be mere drudgery? How can our work be enjoyable without consuming our lives?

Wellness: The Awareness of the Whole Individual

God's Design for Our Work

> "And on the seventh day God finished his work that he had done, and he rested on the seventh day from all his work that he had done." —Genesis 2:2 (ESV)

The earliest chapters of the Bible reveal that our work is an essential part of who we are as men and women created in the image of God. The first chapter of Genesis reveals that God Himself is active—He engages in meaningful work as He creates the world in an orderly fashion that reflects His good purposes. Furthermore, God arranges the world to reveal that we play a central role in His creation. Unlike anything else God creates, human beings are made in the image and likeness of God. As God's image-bearers, men and women were designed to play a unique role in the world—to live out our identities as God's royal sons and daughters.

Two things are essential to understanding God's purpose for us. First, we were created to enjoy a special relationship with God as his children. Second, we were created to govern and steward the world on God's behalf. Think of the world as God's "family business." He entrusts this world to His children to run things for Him. What an incredible privilege!

Because our engagement in the work of the world is a family business, we take our cues from our Heavenly Father. Notice than in Genesis 1:1 to 2:3, God works six days and then rests from His labors. Work is not all that our Father does—He also rests from work. Scripture is clear that God's engagement in both work and rest are a pattern for us to follow. We work as God works, but we also rest from work as God rests. In God's design for us, both work and rest are good and reflect our identity as His children who bear His likeness.

Wellness: The Awareness of the Whole Individual

Things take a turn for the worse, however, in chapter three of Genesis. As a result of our rebellion against our Father, we suffer the consequences for our sin. Notice how the costs of the disobediences of the man and the woman affect our experiences today. Work becomes toilsome. We struggle to meaningfully engage in efforts to produce good and needful things. We face disappointments and setbacks. We get tired and discouraged. Things don't ever seem to come easy for us. In addition, women experience pains in child-bearing. Bringing forth children is a painful experience! And it doesn't end when the delivery is over. Because of the enmity we have toward one another, husbands and wives engage in a power struggle. Parents and children strive with one another for mastery. In other words, both our work and our relationships become sources of suffering in our lives.

Thankfully, that is not the end of the story. From first to last, the Bible reveals that God, in His steadfast love, is determined to rescue His people from all that is wrong with the world. Jesus enters our world on a mission to redeem us from sin and death. Jesus is not only the divine Son of God—He is also the human Son of Man who shows us what it truly means to be sons and daughters of our Heavenly Father. Unlike Adam and Eve, Jesus stays true to God's design for humanity. He comes not to do His own will, but the will of the One who sent Him. He lives out of His likeness to God at every turn.

Jesus tells His people in John 5:19–20, "Truly, truly, I say to you, the Son can do nothing of his own accord, but only what he sees the Father doing. For whatever the Father does, that the Son does likewise. For the Father loves the Son and shows him all that he himself is doing" (ESV). Jesus shows us that in spite of the brokenness of the world, we can still meaningfully engage in the work our Father has for us to do.

Wellness: The Awareness of the Whole Individual

The Dangers of Work

> "No one can serve two masters. Either you will hate the one and love the other, or you will be devoted to the one and despise the other. You cannot serve God and money."
> —Matthew 6:24 (ESV)

It isn't always easy to follow Jesus's example. In our brokenness, we tend to view work in unhealthy ways—sometimes consciously, but just as often unconsciously. Sometimes, we pursue our work with gusto for career advancement and the increased salary it provides. Before long, we find ourselves spending long hours in the office and spending our time at home obsessed with finishing up work projects. We become workaholics, and the all-consuming drive to get ahead puts tremendous strain on our marriages and negatively affects our parenting.

In a previous position, I kept taking on additional projects to impress my boss. The more responsibilities I assumed, the more overwhelmed I began to feel. My anxiety level soon became paralyzing, and I ended up getting reprimanded for not following through on the tasks for which I had volunteered. My desire for approval led me to make foolish decisions that undermined my desire for wellness.

There are other reasons we might focus too much of our time and energy on our work. Some who find family relationships stressful see work as a pleasant escape from the challenges of having those hard conversations with a spouse or child. Or, we may operate under the hidden assumption that the more we achieve, the greater our sense of accomplishment will be and the more self-worth we will feel.

Regardless of the reason, when work begins to take over our lives, we begin to feel more and more trapped. The harder we work, the less satisfying each individual promotion, raise, or accomplishment seems. Work becomes an endless cycle of chasing after the wind for the promised fulfillment we think it offers. To use Jesus's language, work becomes our master, and we become its slave. Sooner or later, we come to realize that no amount of money or accomplishment can ever satisfy the deepest longings of our souls to have value, dignity, and meaningful relationships. Only God can satisfy those longings, and only by pursuing them in Him will we find rest for our souls. As St. Augustine put it, "Thou hast made us for thyself, and our heart is restless until it finds its rest in thee."[5]

On the other hand, we might struggle with apathy toward our work. Today, more and more twenty-somethings find themselves living at home, finding it difficult to get a job and wondering whether they will ever make it on their own. Maybe they don't even really *want* to get a job. The thought of slaving away as part of a corporate machine holds no appeal for them.

It's true that because of the curse in the third chapter of Genesis, our work is toilsome. But because God works, living out our identity as His children means that we, too, must learn to engage in hard work. We were created to reflect God's own productive nature, and when we neglect this responsibility, we unfairly put burdens on others. The apostle Paul stresses this point when he says in 2 Thessalonians 3:10, "If anyone is not willing to work, let him not eat" (ESV).

We may also find it difficult to engage in work if we don't respect our employer. Slacking off seems entirely reasonable when we don't feel like we're being treated fairly. This kind of passive-aggressive attitude doesn't contribute much to our wellness, either. As our resentment builds, we find ourselves being consumed by frustration, bitterness, and anger. So, what is the alternative? How can we experience wellness in the face of unfairness?

Wellness: The Awareness of the Whole Individual

Peter explains how to honor God in such circumstances: "Servants, be subject to your masters with all respect, not only to the good and gentle but also to the unjust. For this is a gracious thing, when, mindful of God, one endures sorrows while suffering unjustly. For what credit is it if, when you sin and are beaten for it, you endure? But if when you do good and suffer for it you endure, this is a gracious thing in the sight of God" (1 Peter 2:18–20, ESV). While we may not be able to escape injustice, we can still honor God in the midst of it, crying out to Him for deliverance and, like Christ, entrusting ourselves to the One who judges justly.

In both extremes (investing too much or too little of ourselves in our work), our livelihoods become enslaving. Either we give ourselves over excessively to our livelihoods, or we rebel against our God-given identity and struggle with anxiety, resentment, or depression. Our wellness depends upon faithfully living out what it means to be the sons and daughters of our Heavenly Father. As we face these temptations in work life, our only hope is to learn to have His perspective in our work.

Working with a Purpose

> "His master replied, 'Well done, good and faithful servant! You have been faithful with a few things; I will put you in charge of many things. Come and share your master's happiness!'" —Matthew 25:21 (NIV)

How, then, should we think about work? In the parable of the talents, Jesus gives us a framework for understanding our relationship to our vocations. In Matthew 25, He describes it in terms of a man who entrusts his property to his servants while he is away. Each of them is given a different sum of money. When the master returns, he expects to find a return on his investment. Regardless of the level of responsibility, he praises the servant who uses what he has given him productively for his master's benefit.

Wellness: The Awareness of the Whole Individual

This idea can be summed up in the word "stewardship." When we see our time, our strengths, and our abilities as things God has entrusted to us to use wisely, then we will likely have the right perspective on our work. We'll understand that our work is not a master we serve, so we won't give ourselves to it looking for ultimate satisfaction. Instead, we'll serve our Heavenly Father by following His example of faithful work along with periods of rest. We'll work knowing that our faithfulness will be rewarded with what every child longs to hear from their parent: "Well done, son. Well done, daughter. I'm so proud of you. Enter into my joy." We'll see our work for what it is—a participation in the family business of God. We'll experience the wellness that comes from meaningful service and satisfying rest.

A Heavenly Vision of Work

> "Whatever you do, work heartily, as for the Lord and not for men, knowing that from the Lord you will receive the inheritance as your reward. You are serving the Lord Christ."
> —Colossians 3:23-24

In his book, *The Curate's Awakening*, George MacDonald describes what work looks like in God's kingdom. He envisions a community where each one uses his or her gifts for the benefit of others. A woman walks into a linen shop, and the shopkeeper selects with great care just the right fabric to make a beautiful dress that will bring out the woman's coloring. Delighted with this gift, she leaves the shop fully satisfied. When asked about why there was no payment, MacDonald explains that no money is necessary in this heavenly vision. Each one simply uses his or her gifts for the benefit of the community. The shopkeeper is free to give away his goods to others, knowing that the bread he needs will be freely given to him by the baker. The one who teaches reading does her work with excellence at no cost, knowing that the homebuilder will ensure that she has a place to live. Whenever anyone feels tempted

Wellness: The Awareness of the Whole Individual

to get more than needed, everyone in the community kneels to pray for strength for that citizen.[6]

This vision of work captures several wonderful things about how God has designed us to live. First, all members of the community understand that they are stewards who have been entrusted with talents and abilities. Not using their gifts for the sake of others would harm the community. Rather, they find a simple pleasure in seeing the joy on the faces of those who benefit from their work. They do their work with excellence, knowing that they are ultimately serving their Heavenly Father when they serve their fellow kingdom citizens. Second, members in the community do not try to accumulate goods or wealth for themselves because they know these things could never truly satisfy their deepest desires. Instead, they are content that their needs will be met. They look for satisfaction in the God who loves them and created them to enjoy Him in their God-given vocation. And third, when members of the community view their work rightly, the whole community flourishes and everyone in it experiences wellness.

Of course, this heavenly vision is an ideal that seems far removed from the brokenness of our lives and our world. In this life, our joys will always come in the midst of sorrows, and our enjoyment of our work will be mixed with the reality of toil. But as we strive toward participating in this world with a heavenly mindset, seeing our work as God sees it, we will know the wellness that comes from living out who we were created to be. As God's sons and daughters, we can experience the joy of faithfully participating in the family business our Heavenly Father has entrusted to us.

Try this self-assessment to see which areas of your life need renewed focus and prayer:

Wellness: The Awareness of the Whole Individual

True	False	God Himself works: He created the world in an orderly fashion to reflect His good purposes
True	False	As God's image bearers, we are designed to work and play a unique role in the world.
True	False	In our brokenness, we tend to view work in unhealthy ways ignoring God's perspective in our work.
True	False	Only God (not our livelihood or accomplishments) can satisfy our longings and help us find rest for our souls.
True	False	We were created to reflect God's own productive nature, and when we neglect this responsibility, we unfairly put burdens on others.
True	False	While we may not be able to escape challenges in our work, we can still honor God in all we do.
True	False	A godly understanding of work encompasses being good stewards entrusted with talents and attributes.
Total ____	Total ____	

Wellness: The Awareness of the Whole Individual

Wellness: The Awareness of the Whole Individual

CHAPTER 5

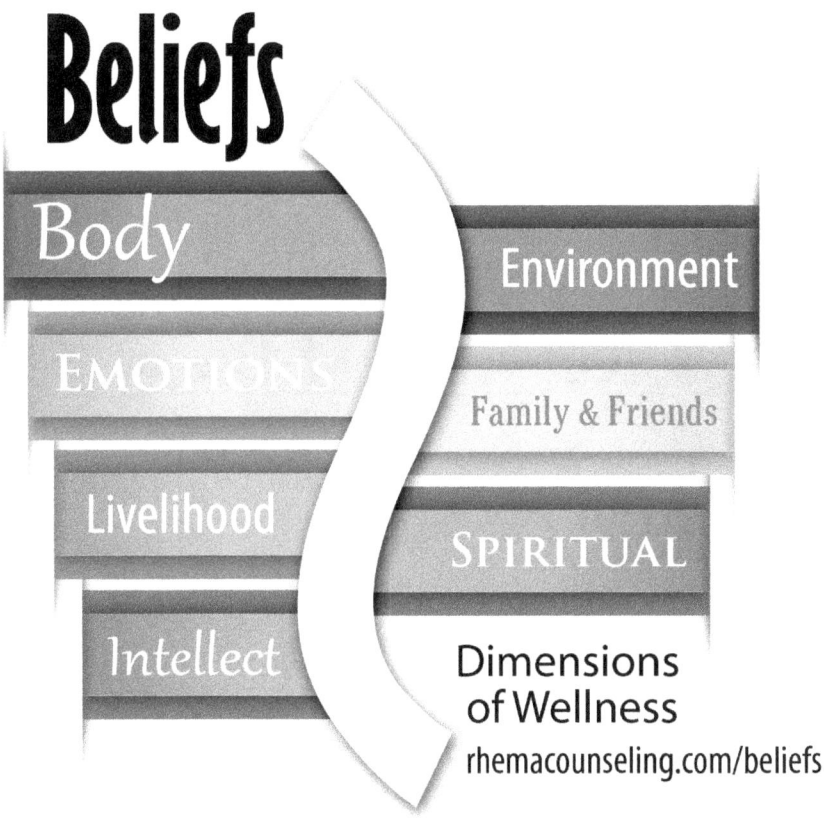

Dimensions of Wellness
rhemacounseling.com/beliefs

Wellness: The Awareness of the Whole Individual

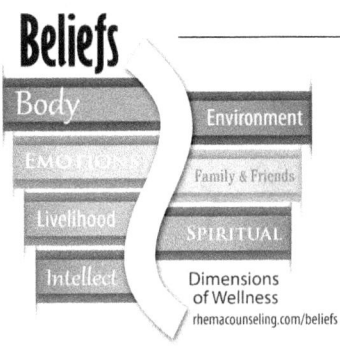

CHAPTER 5

Honoring God with Intellectual Wellness:

A Path to Creative Solutions

by Rickey Hargrave

Wellness is a tough fight but well worth it. Shaping our intellect is important, especially if we want to inculcate the principles of God's Word in our lives.

The concepts of intellect and wellness are not "new age" concepts. These topics have been around since the beginning of recorded history. Can you imagine a more highly developed intellect than that of Adam who named all the animals the Lord God brought to him?

> So the Lord God formed out of the ground every wild animal and every bird of the sky, and brought each to the man to see what he would call it. And whatever the man called a living creature that was its name. The man gave names to all the livestock, to the birds of the sky, and to every wild animal; but for the man no helper was found as his complement. — Genesis 2:19–20 (HCSB)

This chapter will deal with the intellect and intellectual aspects of wellness. We will consider aspects of intellect using studies by various universities, studies on the brain and its development or

Wellness: The Awareness of the Whole Individual

neglect, how each stage of life relates to positive input of mental training, and the direction of scripture to "renew our minds."

Activity and the Word of God

When we discuss the intellect, we include the ability to solve problems, practice creative expression, develop and adopt new ideas, think critically, and explore topics of personal interest. We may not consciously think about accomplishing these things, but they are important in the total development of our intellect, which promotes total wellness.

Intellectual wellness means:

- Keeping an active mind through mental activity and stimulation.
- A demonstrated commitment to lifelong learning.
- Lifelong learning through formal education and informal life experiences.
- Openness to new ideas.
- A capacity to question and think critically.
- Maintaining a sense of creativity and curiosity.
- Being motivated to master new skills and seek out new challenges.
- Challenging the mind with intellectual and creative pursuits.
- Not being self-satisfied and unproductive.
- Being focused on the achievement of a more satisfying existence.

Wellness: The Awareness of the Whole Individual

- A continuous sense of humor, creativity, and curiosity.
- Reaching your own correct decisions when there is a choice or a problem, which is a daily event.
- Making sure the decisions you make are consistent with the scriptures.

In a course titled "Wellness," Butler University lists seven ways to enhance this dimension of our Intellect.

1. Recognize and utilize academic support programs and services as appropriate.
2. Identify educational goals and strive to achieve them.
3. Explore new experiences.
4. Integrate classroom knowledge in day-to-day life and conversations beyond the classroom.
5. Incorporate experiential learning and life lessons both within classroom conversations and beyond.
6. Increase awareness of current events.
7. Cultivate an appreciation for the arts.[7]

Howard University in Columbia, Maryland also gives instruction in Intellectual Wellness. They define it as "being open to new ideas and experiences. It is the desire to continue learning while stimulating and challenging your mind. It is the determination to expand your knowledge and improve your skills for a healthy lifestyle."[8]

The scriptures have many references to keeping the mind working. Clearly, the emphasis in these passages is on the spiritual mandate of meditating on the Word of God and allowing your

Wellness: The Awareness of the Whole Individual

mind to engage the principles of the Almighty. Consider the following passages:

> How can a young man keep his way pure?
> By keeping Your word.
> I have sought You with all my heart;
> don't let me wander from Your commands.
> I have treasured Your word in my heart
> so that I may not sin against You.
> Lord, may You be praised;
> teach me Your statutes.
> With my lips I proclaim
> all the judgments from Your mouth.
> I rejoice in the way revealed by Your decrees
> as much as in all riches.
> I will meditate on Your precepts
> and think about Your ways.
> I will delight in Your statutes;
> I will not forget Your word.
> —Psalm 119:9–16 (HCSB)

> For as he thinketh in his heart, so *is* he... —Proverbs 23:7 (KJV, emphasis added)[9]

> Finally brothers, whatever is true, whatever is honorable, whatever is just, whatever is pure, whatever is lovely, whatever is commendable—if there is any moral excellence and if there is any praise—dwell on these things. Do what you have learned and received and heard and seen in me, and the God of peace will be with you.
> —Philippians 4:8–9 (HCSB)

> Therefore, brothers, by the mercies of God, I urge you to present your bodies as a living sacrifice, holy and pleasing to God; this is your spiritual worship. Do not be conformed to

this age, but be transformed by the renewing of your mind, so that you may discern what is the good, pleasing, and perfect will of God. —Romans 12:1–2 (HCSB)

Cognitive Capabilities or Capacities

When researchers look into brain functions, they consider the scientific and psychological implications. As believers, we do not discount that valuable research. We choose to apply the principles by recognizing the overriding principles in the Word of God.

For instance, C. Miller notes that "fear of losing mental faculties, and perhaps independence, is often considered the worst-case scenario of aging. For some older people, it may trigger near panic when they experience an episode of natural forgetfulness. As we age, a large percentage of older adults will experience minor memory impairments and slower cognitive processing ability. We often use phrases that are negative and demeaning such as 'I am having a senior moment!' or we buy into the lie that 'You can't teach an old dog new tricks.'"[10]

By following the Romans 12 injunction to continually "renew our minds," we recognize that it is important to teach our older generation and their families that age does not mean debilitation. We can constantly keep our minds fresh and alive by thinking on those things the Apostle Paul noted in Philippians 4:8.

Miller also notes, "Intellectual wellness involves engagement in creative and stimulating mental activities, broadening our horizons, opening our minds, using available resources to learn about and discovering the world around us."[11]

A three-decade-long study published in 2003 of Catholic nuns, ages seventy-five to 107, found that those who regularly engaged in games and crosswords were more likely to remain mentally

Wellness: The Awareness of the Whole Individual

alert until death. Nuns who performed more menial tasks, such as housekeeping or kitchen work, did not tend to live as long.[12] While these nuns kept their minds active through games and crosswords, they also spent a large part of their day in meditation and reading the Word of God. We can gather that all nuns meditated and read the Word of God, but those who spent their extra time keeping their minds alert benefited greatly.

Other studies have demonstrated that changes in the brain tend to be individual and are influenced by the interrelated nature of physical, psychosocial, cultural, socioeconomic, spiritual, and environmental aspects.

Observing older adults in my immediate family, I believe they are capable of learning, making judgments, thinking critically, reasoning, and living independently. My paternal grandmother was learning origami at the age of eighty-seven. My wife's maternal grandmother worked the daily crossword from the *Fort Worth Star-Telegram* daily, challenging herself to do it quicker each day.

Studies indicate that there are several positive aspects to the aging brain and, after two decades of research, indicate that "healthy older brains are often as good as or better than younger brains in a wide variety of tasks."[13]

Miller lists five positive aspects of brain development from the academic side:

1. New brain cells form over our lifetime.
2. Experience and learning enable the brain to create new connections.
3. Maturity brings emotional thinking into balance.
4. Analytical and creative tendencies (left and right hemispheres) become more integrated.

Wellness: The Awareness of the Whole Individual

5. Crystallized intelligence (e.g., life learnings) may increase due to experiences and wisdom.[14]

Challenging the Brain for Quality of Life

Intellectual wellness is a critical component that influences overall quality of life. The aging brain and its intellectual capacity must be challenged, or it may deteriorate. Use it, or lose it! Stated another—ancient—way by Hippocrates, "That which is used—develops. That which is not used wastes away."

To help older adults enhance their intellectual wellness, we offer suggestions such as the following:

TIPS FOR IMPROVING BRAIN FITNESS

- Brain stimulation (e.g., games, puzzles)
- Physical exercise (e.g., aerobics, dancing)
- Challenging leisure activities (e.g., solving crossword puzzles, reading, listening to audiobooks)

CONTROL AND MASTERY ACTIVITIES

- Learn a new language or how to play a musical instrument.
- Engage in lifelong learning (e.g., Elderhostel, health education classes, computer skills, surf the internet)

In the past, I have suggested volunteering at a local school or even plowing all the way through *Finnegan's Wake*. If living long and well is your goal, it may be time to act. As the growing body of research suggests, keeping your brain engaged with challenging tasks appears to help stave off cognitive decline, dementia, and Alzheimer's disease. All three of these can lead to premature death and a poor quality of life.

Wellness: The Awareness of the Whole Individual

The National Institute on Aging conducted a seminal study in this area, published in 2002 in the *Journal of the American Medical Association (JAMA)*. Researchers divided 2,800 healthy seniors into three groups. One practiced strategies for remembering lists of words and details in stories. The second worked on reasoning skills, detecting patterns in information and using them to solve problems. The third group tried to boost processing speed by practicing tasks like looking up telephone numbers, reading directions on prescriptions, and responding to traffic signals. Each group showed improved cognitive ability, compared with the baseline, at the end of the ten-week training and again two years later. A control group that received no training experienced no such improvement.

But after you challenge your brain with, say, a word puzzle, it's important to go out and have fun. A 2003 *New England Journal of Medicine* study linked participation in leisure activities like playing musical instruments, dancing, reading, and playing board games with a reduced risk of dementia among seventy-five-year-olds. Researchers theorized that such activities stimulate pleasure-oriented neurotransmitters, forming new connections in the brain.

These studies may challenge you to train your brain to think critically by reading the research in these journal articles appended to this chapter.

Intellectual Challenges of the Younger Generation

If the research vividly clarifies the necessity of keeping the mind sharp throughout the aging process, what about the intellectual wellness of our children? Scripture is clear that the obligation of teaching and training the child belongs to the parent. We will look at scripture to see what guiding principles exist there.

Wellness: The Awareness of the Whole Individual

Teach a youth about the way he should go; even when he is old he will not depart from it. —Proverbs 22:6 (HCSB)

Only be on your guard and diligently watch yourselves, so that you don't forget the things your eyes have seen and so that they don't slip from your mind as long as you live. Teach them to your children and your grandchildren.
—Deuteronomy 4:9 (HCSB)

Imprint these words of mine on your hearts and minds, bind them as a sign on your hands, and let them be a symbol on your foreheads. Teach them to your children, talking about them when you sit in your house and when you walk along the road, when you lie down and when you get up. Write them on the doorposts of your house and on your gates, so that as long as the heavens are above the earth, your days and those of your children may be many in the land the Lord swore to give your fathers.
—Deuteronomy 11:18–21 (HCSB)

Applying Intellectual Precepts

The principles are very clear. Teach the children in the way they should go. We should teach them the things of God, principles of love, morality, family, and faith. As we teach them, their minds focus on the Lord. We use many different methods of teaching including, in our day, books, nature, games, puzzles, and activities. Many publishing houses have materials that are effective for teaching little ones.

When they get older, the wisdom of the parents is passed down to them. I know it helped me to understand my place. My dad used to say, "Rickey, if you do not want to fall down, stay out of slippery places." He went on to tell me of the dangers of alcoholic beverages, smoking, and not maintaining purity in my life.

Wellness: The Awareness of the Whole Individual

In a recent sermon, I quoted an excerpt from Charles R. Kelley's book *Dreamer to Dream Maker*. He said fifteen college professors who taught on the topic of *motivation* were asked to prepare concise statements on the subject. After hours of work, they came up with this:

What the mind attends to it considers.
And what it does not attend to it dismisses.
What the mind attends to continually it believes.
What the mind believes it eventually does.[15]

So, Proverbs 23:7 tells us that "as a man thinketh in his heart, so is he." By keeping the laws of God before our minds and those of our children, we can imprint them on their hearts. Now, Psalm 119 comes into play.

The confidence of knowing the principles of the Word of God from a very early age can mold a mind and strengthen a resolve as nothing else can. Wellness through renewing the mind is very much at work here.

Repetition with children at a young age is important as they grow into teenagers, as Dr. Frances Jensen shows in the book *The Teenage Brain*.[16] Dr. Jensen is a single mother who raised two boys, now in their twenties. She is chair of the Department of Neurology at the University of Pennsylvania Perelman School of Medicine. She wanted to learn why teenagers were so impulsive, moody, and not very good at responsible decision-making. She believes the culprit is the frontal lobe, which takes a long time to develop. Her book goes into the deleterious effects of drugs, alcohol, constant negative stimuli, and even cell phone usage.

By repeating and reinforcing proper behavior, love, and education, the excitement of learning can be the stimuli necessary to shape proper behavior.

Wellness: The Awareness of the Whole Individual

We note scripture once again in Proverbs 22:6: "Teach a youth about the way he should go; even when he is old he will not depart from it" (HCSB).

Wellness in our children and in our teenagers is a tough fight but well worth it. Shaping their intellect is important, especially if we want to inculcate the principles of God's Word in them.

Try this self-assessment to see which areas of your life need renewed focus and prayer:

True	False	I have treasured God's word in my heart and I meditate on His precepts. (Psalm 119:9-16)
True	False	I participate in creative and stimulating mental activities regularly.
True	False	I use many available resources to learn about and discover the world around me.
True	False	I remain open to new ideas and experiences.
True	False	I am determined to expand my knowledge and improve my skills for a healthy lifestyle.
True	False	Scripture is clear that the obligation of teaching and training the child belongs to the parent.
True	False	I strive to enhance the intellectual stimulation of my children in many ways.
Total ____	Total ____	

Wellness: The Awareness of the Whole Individual

Wellness: The Awareness of the Whole Individual

CHAPTER 6

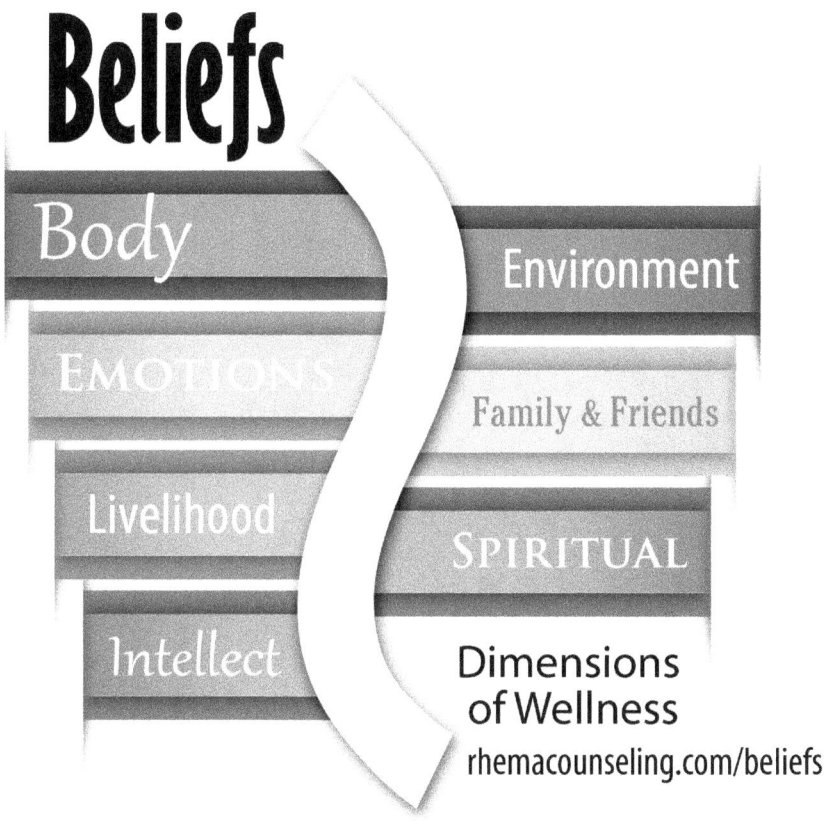

Dimensions of Wellness
rhemacounseling.com/beliefs

Wellness: The Awareness of the Whole Individual

CHAPTER 6

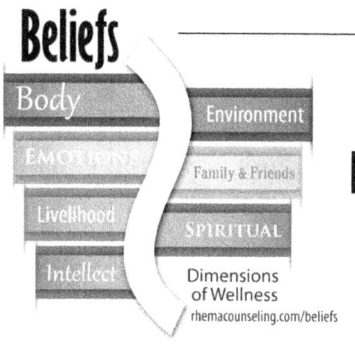

Honoring God with Environmental Wellness:

Warning—Toxic Environment!

by Audrey Werner

We need God—now more than ever—to heal our land, but I believe it begins with us cleaning up our own acts first before we can help others. Get rid of those toxins!

While in high school, I did not have a car, so I was reduced to riding the bus with all the other "un-cool" kids. I attended a small Christian high school, which was several miles away, so my ride was long and boring for the most part. However, I was always intrigued by a very large garbage dump site we would pass on the bus route. The previous owner had allowed toxic waste to be dumped on the site, and these toxins were so dangerous that the entire site had to be fenced off with signs posted all around it featuring the skull and crossbones symbol and the words "toxic waste site—do not enter."

We hear often of toxins in our environment. The dawn of the Industrial Revolution brought factories and innovation. Unfortunately, the byproducts of these factories were toxins that seeped into the soil, into the air, into the water supplies, and, in certain areas, even into our food sources.

We are learning how toxins can kill us and how we need to clean up the physical environment around us. The wellness industry has

Wellness: The Awareness of the Whole Individual

exploded over the last thirty years as we are learning how to avoid toxins and detox in order to prevent diseases and cancers.

One of the ways we promote wellness is by teaching others how to clean up another type of toxin: the spiritual toxins in our environment. There are spiritual toxins we will discuss that can contribute to a toxic environment: "words spoken" and "images viewed" and "acts of abuse."

Let's talk about the word "environment." Webster's 1828 dictionary—the very first one—was written to define every word in the King James Bible so we would not lose the rich meaning of each word. Interestingly, the word "environment" is not in this book, but the word "environ," the root word of "environment," is there. It is defined as, "to surround, to encompass, and to encircle." The definition also includes this secondary definition: "to involve, to envelop; *as to environ with darkness, or with difficulties*" (emphasis added).[17]

Skipping forward to a more recent dictionary, the word "environment," is defined as, "external conditions which determine modifications in the development of organic life."[18] According to this definition, the environments we are in—especially those that are toxic—can affect how we develop.

A Word about Physical Environments

> Their land is also full of idols; they worship the work of their own hands, that which their own fingers have made.
> —Isaiah 2:8

Let's talk about the actual physical space that we occupy. Take a look around at your dwelling. What does your space look like? How many "idols" might be cluttering up your living quarters? This can be a toxic environment.

Wellness: The Awareness of the Whole Individual

When I began my career in Public Health Nursing, I was assigned to a large inner city community. The homes I visited were homes of those who lived in poverty, homes of those who were depressed, and homes of drug dealers and addicts. I remember one home in particular that was so cluttered the owner asked to meet with me on her front porch. As we sat and visited, a rat peered out the window from inside the home. I was horrified to think that someone could possibly live in such an environment.

The environment in which we live can affect our safety, health, and development. Now I am hoping that as we look around at our living quarters, we are not confronted with a rat, but with clutter, dirt, and disorganization in our physical environment! Could a change in our physical environment affect our outcome, our mood, and our mental health?

Our family had a "dump room" in the house. This was a room where we dumped all our unwanted furniture, pictures, and boxes that didn't fit anywhere else. We even had a 12 foot Pacific Blue Marlin hanging on the wall in this room because we had nowhere else to put her. A very godly woman by the name of Susan Morrow, who happened to be an interior decorator, offered to help me re-organize one day. We purged; we removed all the boxes, rearranged or got rid of some of the furniture and even moved the fish to the garage. Susan donated a painting called, "The Gathering Place" to this room and I have to tell you the results were phenomenal.

When I entered the "dump" I was angry at the clutter, depressed at the sight, and I was ashamed to show anyone that part of the house. I couldn't concentrate while surrounded by this mess and never did any work in that room. Now, this room has become a haven: an office where I teach an on-line class, a living room where I meet with fellow Christian women to visit and pray, and a conference room where I can strategize with friends and volunteers to run my ministry—The Matthew XVIII Group. I feel empowered in this room.

The Toxic Tongue: The Power of Spoken Words

> A wholesome tongue is a tree of life, but perverseness in it breaks the spirit. —Proverbs 15:4 (NKJV)

Negative words that are spoken on a daily basis can be toxic for those around us. Hearing such words as "You are stupid," "You are too fat," "You will never succeed," and, "You are just a follower, not a leader," are all statements that can "environ with darkness" or crush the spirit of any individual.

Sexual words can also be powerful and influential. For example, sex education was formerly introduced into the public arena in 1964 based on the premise that children are "sexual from birth" and in need of graphic sex information.[19] Once sex education became legal, secular organizations were there to help form the words to share in classrooms across the country and from 1964 to 1972 there was a sharp increase in teen pregnancy and sexually transmitted diseases and this trend has continued to present day.[20]

Another group of dangerous words can include profanity. Profanity can be damaging when uttered to others in anger. God warns us in Exodus 20:7, "You shall not take the name of the Lord your God in vain, for the Lord will not hold him guiltless who take His name in vain" (NKJV). One author in 1890 spoke of the dangers of profanity, "It seems to destroy the finest of sensibilities, the best of affections and generous feelings."[21]

In Matthew 12:36–37, Jesus said, "But I say to you that for every idle word men may speak, they will give account of it in the Day of Judgment. For by your words you will be justified and by your words you will be condemned" (NKJV). We will be accountable for the words that come from our mouths, and we can either build up or tear down others with the words that we use.

Toxic Images Lead to Corruption

> Professing themselves to be wise, they became fools, and changed the glory of the incorruptible God into an image made like corruptible man-and birds and four footed animals and creeping things. —Romans 1:22-23

Another type of environmental toxin that profoundly and negatively impacts us is violent and sexual imagery, which is everywhere, thanks to the removal of laws against obscenity and the explosion of the pornography industry, beginning in 1953 with the first issue of *Playboy*.[22] Through these images, we have been taught that murder in many different graphic ways may be acceptable in some cases, and we are taught to pursue the lust of the flesh. We have been taught, "If it feels good, do it," and "what I do behind closed doors affects no one else," through the movies and television shows we watch, the sex education programs we go through in school, and through pornography, which is now available and easily accessible to people of all ages.

I am a former Public Health Nurse who worked in the Sexually Transmitted Disease (STD) Clinic. In the mid-1990s, we saw a dramatic upsurge of date rape cases. Women who had been raped on a date were coming to us to make sure they did not contract an STD. I never understood why the upsurge happened until I saw a documentary on the pornography industry in 2002. It seems that in the early 1990s, legal restrictions were removed and the pornography industry exploded. In pornography, the typical theme is that man is the predator and women are the prey. Men were viewing this imagery and acting out what they saw. Imagery is powerful, dangerous, and toxic.

Wellness: The Awareness of the Whole Individual

Since 1953 with the first issue of *Playboy*, men have been taught through words and images to look at women not as wives, daughters, aunts, or grandmothers, but as "Playmates." Men are not taught to protect women but to prey upon them. Women are being taught through words and images to reject romance and welcome bondage and torture from men. Rape of children has also exploded as we are fed images and words of adults having sex with teens and sometimes children through movies, television, and books.[23]

Dr. Judith Reisman is considered one of the leading authorities on the Sexual Revolution, and she has done extensive research on the effects of graphic sexual imagery on the brain. She states, "When judges freed obscenity, toxic media, from control, post-1948, excitatory transmitters were also liberated from control, documenting increasing sexual and transsexual abuse of women and children."[24] In 1984, Neil Malamuth and James Check reported on a study in which they showed UCLA college males a series of films depicting acts of sexual violence. Prior to viewing the films, the students had expressed normal, non-violent sexual attitudes. After the films, more than half of the college men claimed they would rape a woman—if they were sure they would not get caught.[25]

What we view and what we hear affects what we think about ourselves and others. In this sex-saturated culture, we are getting further away from God's design for us as men and women in Christ. We believe what we have been told, and as sexual sin—or, the "lust of the flesh"—has been sold to us as the ultimate gift, we have been left with broken relationships, deteriorating families, a more hostile culture, and a nation on moral decline. This reminds me of this scripture: "Her house [the adulteress] is the way to Sheol, going down to the chambers of death (Proverbs 7:27 ESV).

The Toxic Environment of Abuse

> Love is patient and kind; love does not envy or boast; it is not arrogant or rude. It does not insist on its own way; it is not irritable or resentful; it does not rejoice at wrongdoing, but rejoices with truth. Love bears all things, believes all things, hopes all things, endures all things.
> —1 Corinthians 13:4-7 (ESV)

Unfortunately, sexual and physical abuse is on the rise in this nation.[26] When someone says that they love a person but follow up their words with actions of abuse, this is clearly not love. I often take young people to the above scripture so they see what Biblical love looks like and the opposite characteristics would give one a picture of lust. For example, if love is patient, lust is in a hurry, and so on.

If we are in an abusive environment, we need to know that no one deserves abuse. We always recommend that anyone being abused should seek wise counsel immediately. God has a plan for your life and it is a plan for a hope and a future (Jeremiah 29:4) and not abuse and pain.

The Times, They Are A-Changin'!

> And do not be conformed to this world, but be transformed by the renewing of your mind, that you may prove what *is* that good and acceptable and perfect will of God. —Romans 12:2 (NKJV)

> And have no fellowship with the unfruitful works of darkness, but rather expose them. —Ephesians 5:11 (NKJV)

We have changed as a society over the past few decades as we have embraced the words and images around us. According to the

Wellness: The Awareness of the Whole Individual

Barna survey done every year, the rates of single-parent homes, divorces, sexual abuse, and suicide continue to rise.[27] I propose that our environment has something to do with the trends we are seeing. Spiritual toxins are seeping into individuals and their families, bringing darkness and wreaking havoc.

Many people are in therapy today not just because of things that were done to them in their childhoods, but also because of the words that were spoken to them. Words that tear down, words that children believe can define who they are in their own minds: "Who would want to be around you," "You are weak," "You are not loved or wanted," or even, "If you don't behave, I will send you back to _____."

As society seems to be removing God and His standards from our laws, schools and even churches in some cases, we are moving toward darker times. Words, images, and the physical surroundings are affecting individuals in a detrimental way; however we have the power to change our environment. It is time to create a healthy environment for generations to come!

We Can Create Pure Environments!

I can do all things through Christ who strengthens me!
—Philippians 4:13

If we identify that we do indeed have a few physical and spiritual toxins in our lives, there are some creative things we can do about it.

First, humble yourself and pray for clarity from the Lord as to what those toxins are. Some will be obvious, and some will not. God can reveal them to you if you spend time with Him in prayer. I am always amazed when people come to me with a problem and I ask them if they have talked to God about it and they answer "no."

I encourage them to take their problems to God in prayer. Many times, they will return to me astonished that God resolved the problem or gave them clarity in their situation. One woman even said to me, "I should have tried this first instead of last!"

In 2 Chronicles 7:14, God reminds us, "If My people who are called by My name will humble themselves, and pray and seek My face, and turn from their wicked ways, then I will hear from heaven, and will forgive their sin and heal their land" (NKJV). Many Christians have not taken the time to lay prostrate before the Lord, humbled in prayer and seeking His face. We need Him—now more than ever—to heal our land, but I believe it begins with us cleaning up our own acts first before we can help others. Get rid of those toxins!

Second, read God's Word daily! The Word states in Galatians 5:16, "Walk in the Spirit, and you shall not fulfill the lust of the flesh" (NKJV), which means that if we bathe our minds with God's Word, we can turn from the toxic images and words in our environment. Psalm 119:105 says, "Thy Word is a lamp unto my feet and a light unto my path" (NKJV). When you turn on the light, the darkness disappears! We need to be filling our minds with the light and not the darkness of the world.

Next, turn off all media (movies, TV, personal devices other than for work) for a week or two, and see what happens! What TV show or movie have you seen in the last week that was not honoring God? I would guess that if you live in America, it would be very difficult to choose just one. Even watching the news can lead to a commercial about an upcoming show that reveals and glorifies sexual sin. Tune out the world, be in prayer, and read God's Word and see what happens! A few years ago, I was in a women's Bible study which required me to do a lot of homework. The instructor had wisely encouraged us to avoid media for a week, so I purposely did not watch TV or listen to the radio. I

Wellness: The Awareness of the Whole Individual

was surprised with what happened next; it seemed as if I could suddenly hear God every day. Scripture verses jumped off the page and seemed to be exactly what I needed to hear at that time in my life. The results of avoiding the media for a week were astonishing; I was more at peace and I felt confidence in being a child of God in a lost world.

Finally, if you have a sound biblical advisor, accountability partner, or friend to whom you can talk, ask them to help you identify spiritual toxins in your life. Sometimes, those who are close to you can see things you cannot. Proverbs 9:9 states, "Give instruction to a wise man, and he will be still wiser; teach a just man, and he will increase in learning" (NKJV). It is always a good thing to receive godly counsel and be accountable to other Christians.

So, the question is, do you live in a physically and spiritually toxic environment? I want you to pause and look at what surrounds you in your home and work place. God calls us to be separate or different from the world. Do you blend in with the toxic environment, or do you stand out? Are you honoring God in what is before your eyes or with what is coming out of your mouth?

If you note you have a toxic physical or spiritual environment, then clean it up! Remember, "I can do all things through Christ who strengthens me" (Philippians 4:13, NKJV). Looking at our nation today, I'd say we have our work cut out for us!

We Can Clean Up Our Toxic Environments!

> Do not love the world or the things in the world. If anyone loves the world, the love of the Father is not in him. For all that *is* in the world—the lust of the flesh, the lust of the eyes, and the pride of life—is not of the Father but is of the world. And the world is passing away, and the lust of it; but he who does the will of God abides forever. —1 John 2:15–17 (NKJV)

Wellness: The Awareness of the Whole Individual

So, what is surrounding you on a daily basis? What is affecting your life? Are there some physical or spiritual toxins that need to be removed from your home that are causing pain and suffering?

Here are a few assessment statements to help you determine if you live in an environment free of toxins:

True	False	My physical environment is clean and uncluttered.
True	False	I look forward to going home to my living quarters.
True	False	I focus on using positive words with those in my environment.
True	False	I receive positive words from those in my environment.
True	False	My environment is free from any sexual images (music, television, computer, magazines and books).
True	False	I live in and promote an environment that displays Biblical love.
True	False	I am safe and free from physical and sexual abuse.
Total ____	Total ____	

If you affirmed a resounding "yes" to all the above statements, you can determine that your home is pure. However, if you answered "no" to any of the statements above, be aware that you live in a toxic spiritual environment that can cause harm to you or to your family.

Wellness: The Awareness of the Whole Individual

Wellness: The Awareness of the Whole Individual

CHAPTER 7

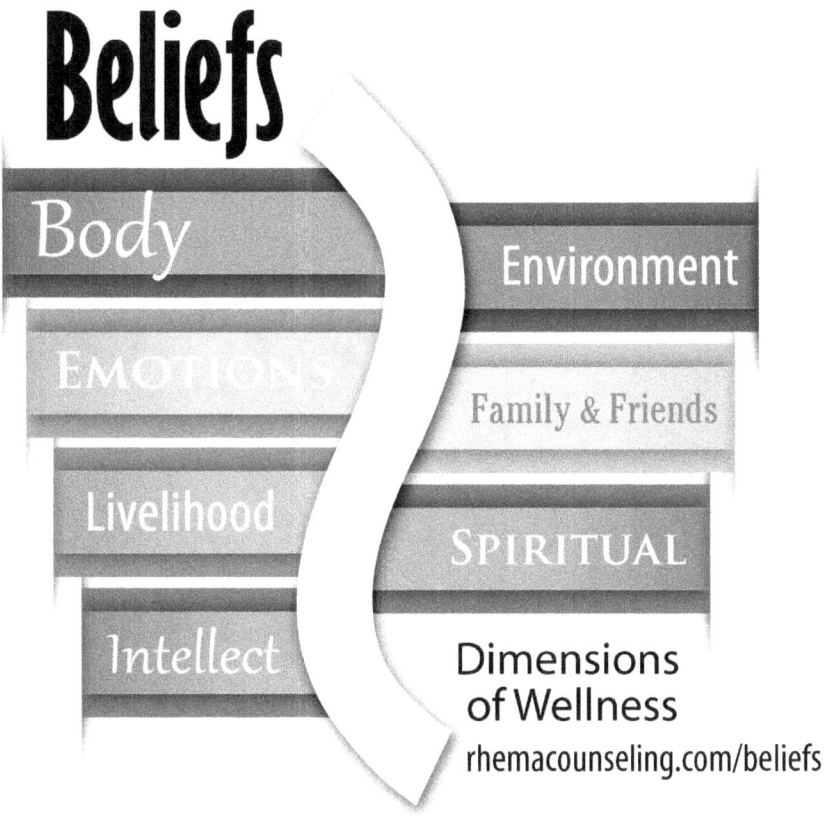

CHAPTER 7

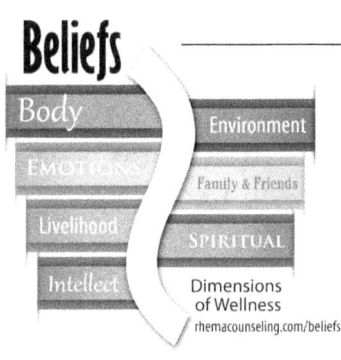

Honoring God with Relational Wellness:

Connectedness Fosters Wholeness

by Grace Edoho-ukwa

A person standing alone can be attacked and defeated, but two can stand back-to-back and conquer.

Loneliness hampers wellness, and connecting with family and friends facilitates well-being. Genesis 2:18 says, "Then the Lord God said, 'It is *not* good for the man to be alone'" (NLT, emphasis added).

In the history of the creation of heaven and earth, God spoke different aspects of His creation into existence for five days, and at the end of each day, He looked back and said "it was good." At the end of day six, after He had completed all His work, 'God looked over all He had made, and He saw that it was *very good*!" (Genesis 1:31 NLT, emphasis added). In the midst His very good creation, God looked at the man he created and gave dominion over all things and saw the first thing that was "not good;" the man was alone. The man, Adam, was in harmony with his environment. He could relate to the animals and everything around him, but God saw him as "alone" and said it was "not good."

After God spoke everything into existence, He lovingly created Adam, breathed His own life into him, and maintained a loving

Wellness: The Awareness of the Whole Individual

relationship with him. The all-knowing God—who intensely abhors sin—knew how much man would sin against Him. Instead of separating man from His love, He graciously made provision to restore him, through the Blood of His dear Son, to Himself. Even while Adam was in this great relationship, God saw Adam as "alone" and in need of a relationship with someone exactly like Him.

We Were Created to Be In Relationship

If, in God's plan of creation, man had to be in relationship with Him and with his fellow man, how can our wellness be complete if we neglect either of these relationships?

In Mark 12:29–31, on the issue of the greatest commandment, Jesus responded to the scribe as follows:

> "The most important one," answered Jesus, "is this: 'Hear, O Israel: The Lord our God, the Lord is one. Love the Lord your God with all your heart and with all your soul and with all your mind and with all your strength.' The second is this: 'Love your neighbor as yourself.' There is no commandment greater than these." (NIV)

Because we were created to be in relationship with God first and then with one another, we cannot function in our full potential in isolation. There is a natural void in us if we do not connect with God and with others around us. Since these relationships are such an essential part of our being, every change in them has great power to alter our well-being in the direction of the change. Our well-being is enhanced when we are well-connected with God and with those around us and diminished when there is a disconnect in any of these relationships.

We have a rewarding relationship with one another when we can relate with God.

Wellness: The Awareness of the Whole Individual

We are affected emotionally in our interpersonal relationships, especially in the relationships with those closest to us. Healthy relationships with those around us enhance wellness in most areas of our lives. An unhealthy relationship hinders wellness, and disconnecting completely from those closest to us creates a void that perpetually deters wellness. There is innate potential and desire in us to connect with those in our systems. As seen in creation, God desires for man to connect with Him first (vertical relationship) and then with one another (horizontal relationship). When we are effective in our vertical relationship, then we obtain the ability to function effectively in our horizontal relationships and have more rewarding bonds with our neighbors.

Every individual is a part of a larger system and functions in full potential when he is able to operate as a member of his system—beginning from the smallest unit, the family, to the community, and on to the rest of humanity. We feel genuinely secure and whole when we connect and have a sense of belonging to the people around us. It becomes necessary for us to be a part of—and in harmony with—our families, friends, and our community to have total wellness.

What is the Family?

McGrath defined the family as "a unit ordained by God for the comfort and protection of its members."[28] Oxford Dictionary defines the family as "a group of people related to one another by blood or by marriage" or "a person or people related to one and so to be treated with a special loyalty or intimacy."[29]

From the definitions, we know "family" could be formed by blood, marriage, or simply people brought together by God as He pleases. But whichever way they come together, there is something to unite and make them a *people*. The words "comfort" and "protection," as well as "special loyalty or intimacy," speak of a

Wellness: The Awareness of the Whole Individual

family as a unit with members deeply concerned about the welfare of each other.

Are all family members loyal to one another? Is there intimacy and comfort in all families? Is every person in a family willing to protect other members with all they have? These are a few essential ideals that bring persistent connection among family members. A few other words that come to mind when I think about family are: sharing, caring, nursing, nurturing, providing, guiding, talking, teasing, laughing, praising, listening, appeasing, calming, coaxing, debating, arguing, bickering, stressing, fighting, worrying, crying, holding, hugging, and bonding. So many delicious words and so many not-so-sweet, which shows that a well-rounded family combines enormously good qualities with assets that are less desirable. There are good times and bad times, and families are in constant movement through different seasons. How we handle the changes that accompany these seasons determines the level of our wellness.

In good or not-so-good seasons, we cannot escape the innate need in us to belong and the persistent desire to form attachments. According to Nikelly, "Human nature involves the drive to form positive, stable, and lasting interpersonal relationships characterized by mutual caring and concern for each other's well-being. Social bonds increase chances for survival, and attachment to groups protects against danger."[30] Minuchin states; "Man is not an isolate. He is an acting and reacting member of a social group. What he experiences as real depends on both internal and external components."[31] We naturally have a deep desire to belong, and since, in belonging, we have to relate with others who are not exactly like us, that desire in us may or may not be fulfilled by how we choose to react to others' actions.

Live in Peace with Everyone

As humans, it is natural for us to react to the actions of those around us, and because our innate tendency is to bond, our reactions can affect our wellness immensely. Colapinto saw the family as an open system and stated, "As an open system the family is subjected to and impinges on the surrounding environment. This implies that family members are not the only architects of their family shape; relevant rules may be imposed by the immediate group of reference or by the culture in the broader sense."[32] Family members are not only influenced by what occurs within the family, but also by a lot of societal occurrences. This may be one reason we see peculiar actions by family members that cannot be explained. We cannot control the actions of others, but we have the ability to control our own reactions. Because we desire relationships, we should choose reactions that may foster connectedness and enhance our wellness.

In Romans 12:18; the Apostle Paul states, "If it is possible, as far as it depends on you, live at peace with everyone" (NIV). The appeal here is for us to choose to offer the gift of peace to ourselves first and then to others in the face of upheavals in our relationships. Essentially, Paul is referring to the fact that in a normal family with minimal dysfunctions, every individual is different with different needs and priorities, so there is need for members to be able to accommodate one another.

Families are characterized by uniquely different dynamics and are constantly moving through changes influenced by the family, the life cycles, and some effects of daily living. These include marriages, new births, children leaving home, aging, illnesses, attending to aging parents, and deaths. These various changes tend to affect members positively or negatively at different levels. Family members can hold together and grow, members can be indifferent, or the family can break up. It is possible to work

Wellness: The Awareness of the Whole Individual

together to resolve difficult situations resulting in a stronger unit, but sometimes it is difficult for some issues to be resolved, and members may walk away with heavy hearts unable to forgive. Anger and the inability to forgive creates a void in us and hinders our wellness. We can work to resolve these issues quickly and avoid the possibility of transferring these feelings to others. A person in isolation has blocked wellness. A life in isolation is not the perfect life, and it's not the will of God for you.

Sharing Your Loads Reduces the Weight of Burdens

> This is the case of a man who is all alone, without a child or a brother, yet who works hard to gain as much wealth as he can. But then he asks himself, "Who am I working for? Why am I giving up so much pleasure now?" It is all so meaningless and depressing. Two people are better off than one, for they can help each other succeed. If one person falls, the other can reach out and help. But someone who falls alone is in real trouble. Likewise, two people lying close together can keep each other warm. But how can one be warm alone? A person standing alone can be attacked and defeated, but two can stand back-to-back and conquer. Three are even better, for a triple-braided cord is not easily broken.
> —Ecclesiastes 4:8–12 (NLT)

It is so ironic that King Solomon described this as depressing. Most people who prefer a life of solitude occupy themselves with their jobs. Most of them have very little to do with their "dysfunctional" family members and not much use for friends because that just opens up an opportunity for betrayal. Some people are only concerned about their pets and believe these are the ones who will love no matter what. Is it possible that this assumption holds because pets can never speak their minds? What if, like with Balaam and the dumb donkey, your pet could speak just once and tell you what others see in you—would it still be your best friend? Pets are very good companions, but can they speak for you? Can they inherit the wages of your hard labor? When you are depressed, it may help to hear a voice similar to yours.

The King stated, "Two people are better off than one, for they can help each other succeed." How heavy is your load? How would it feel to have extra support at the other end?

It is a common practice in rural areas of Africa, were I was raised, to have young ladies go and gather firewood and bring it home in bundles. As a young girl growing up, I was allowed to go with my friends every now and then. This was a chore that I looked forward to and enjoyed. It was a lot of fun talking, singing, and dancing on the way and even while gathering the wood with so many friends.

Returning with the load on my head was never that much fun. The group was always delayed because the smaller girls would need a break, and every one would have to put down their loads and wait. The big girls decided to put our loads together, taught us how to walk in sync, and then had two or three girls carry each load—one at each end and maybe one person in the middle. Even though the weight remained the same, the loads felt much lighter, and it was fun having to walk in sync. We could sing and even dance when returning.

From working with individuals and families, I have seen that there is relief in sharing burdens, but if you isolate yourself from family and friends, how do you share and lessen your burdens? The King talked about how if you fall, it is much harder to get back on your feet alone than if a friend's outstretched hands are there. Even knowing you are not alone gives you so much strength. Regardless of the nature of your "fall," you can be encouraged by the ones on your side, no matter how little they can offer. A "fall" can be an impairment, a block, a drawback, a weakness, or inhibition in any area of your wellness. Since we were created to be in relationships

Wellness: The Awareness of the Whole Individual

with others, we can rise up much easier with the support of those around us and even more so when we are in sync with them.

Remember, "A person standing alone can be attacked and defeated, but two can stand back-to-back and conquer." What is attacking you in life? Is the attack physical, emotional, or spiritual? If you are alone when you are attacked, there is a great possibility that you will be defeated. You gain strength when you have someone fighting by your side.

Who Can Fight by Your Side?

Ephesians 4:2 says, "Always be humble and gentle. Be patient with each other, making allowance for each other's faults because of your love" (NLT).

We are uniquely created with individual characteristics different from all others, yet God intended that we live together and accommodate each other's differences. A person with a gentle and humble spirit has the potential to accommodate family members, even through difficult times. To make allowance for others' faults means you already know that there are obvious blemishes in people—and more that will be discovered in the future—but you are not discouraged by these blemishes. You have enough forgiveness available to offer, along with help as needed. You step aside when necessary, but you do not isolate.

It may be necessary at some point to have some distance between blood relatives, but it is best that this is done peacefully so a huge bridge is not created that could permanently prevent contact. A healthy boundary is necessary in a family, not a bridge. Sometimes, when there is a disconnect between blood relatives, God may bring friends and even strangers to ensure no void is created. Keep and treasure every person who comes into your life. God has them there at that moment to fulfill His purpose. Proverbs

Wellness: The Awareness of the Whole Individual

27:10 states, "Never abandon a friend—either yours or your father's. When disaster strikes, you won't have to ask your brother for assistance. It's better to go to a neighbor than to a brother who lives far away" (NLT).

Allow Yourself Room for Healing

If you cannot get to your brother, have access to your friend; do not block everyone from your life for fear of getting hurt or for any other reason. Do not live perpetually in your painful past. Allow room for healing, and make it a brighter future. Forgive; this is your gift to yourself. Mend mendable broken relationships. Give yourself peace, and offer the same to others.

The most beautiful house can be very cold and meaningless if you have no one to share the beauty. It can be loathsome with a quarrelsome companion, and a delight when it is filled with love, peace, and laughter. If you have a warm, comfortable place to go at the end of your workday, you have a home. If people are waiting in this beautiful place to share your love, you have a family. If there is peace and you long to return here every day, your wellness will be enhanced in this place. Proverbs 22:19 says, "Better to live in a desert than with a quarrelsome and nagging wife."

Since we are acting and reacting to members of our families, we can affect our family members in very powerful but unpredictable ways, just as they can affect us. As a counselor, I am aware of the fact that the source of most human suffering is the effect of present or past relationships, but I'm also aware of the fact that how we respond in these relationships has a great impact on our wellness. As we desire peace from relatives, we should endeavor to give them peace. If we seek peace and pursue it as the Bible advised, and there is still no peace at home, at least we can refuse to fight back so there will be fewer conflicts within the family. Give to your family and friends what you desire from them, and when they

Wellness: The Awareness of the Whole Individual

give back, you will enjoy their gift even more, and you will have contentment and wellness from your relationships.

You must be the change you wish to see in the world.
—Mahatma Gandhi

Try this assessment:

True	False	I have family and friends around me.
True	False	It is peaceful and not quarrelsome in my family.
True	False	I have contentment in my relationship with my family members.
True	False	I am a gift to my family members.
True	False	My family members are a gift to me.
True	False	My family members accept me for who I am and love me no matter what.
True	False	My family is a small world created and surrounded by love.
Total ___	Total ___	

Wellness: The Awareness of the Whole Individual

CHAPTER 8

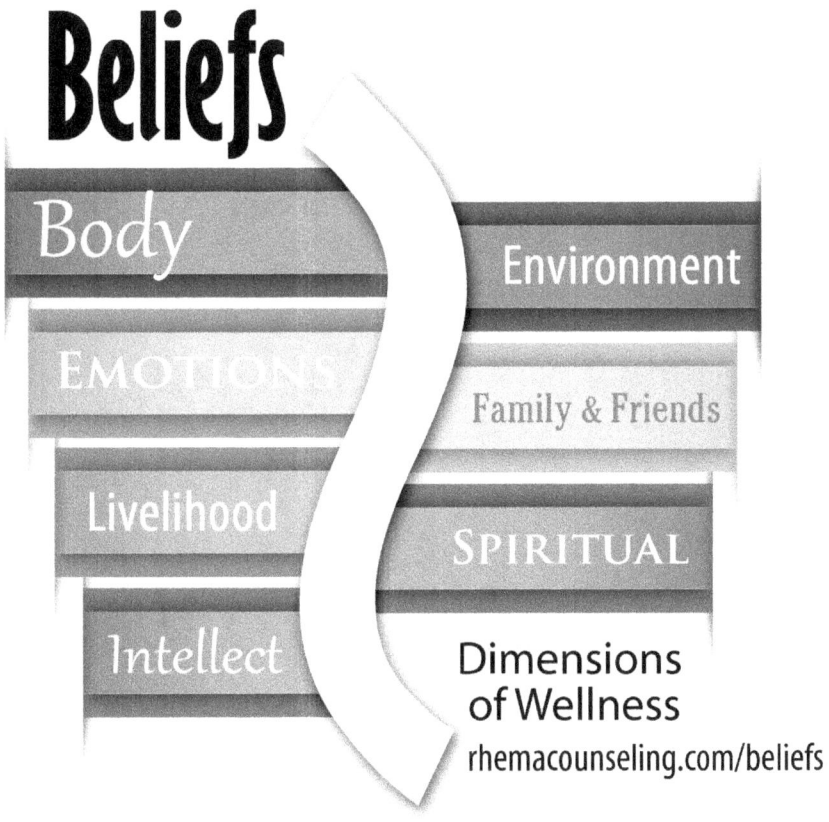

Dimensions of Wellness
rhemacounseling.com/beliefs

Wellness: The Awareness of the Whole Individual

CHAPTER 8

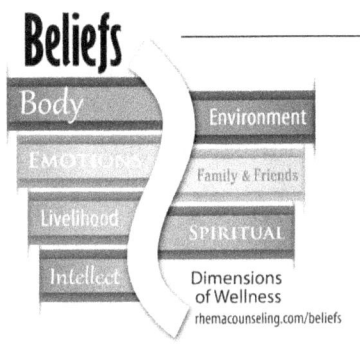

Honoring God with Spiritual Wellness:

Growing into Godliness!

by Karen Lindwall-Bourg

We are not human beings having a spiritual experience. We are spiritual beings having a human experience.
—Pierre Teilhard de Chardin

Even though the word "wellness" is not found in the Bible, God has a great deal to say about it.

His desire for us is to experience perfect health and well-being in the form of optimal physical, emotional, intellectual, environmental, social, spiritual, and occupational and financial wellness. For example, God wants us physically healed and free from sickness and disease.[33] Emotionally, He wants us to be fulfilled, to live with purpose, and to live the abundant life.[34] He wants us to know love, joy, peace, and all the products of a life directed by the Holy Spirit. He wants us to be free from worry and stress, even in the midst of trials and tribulations.[35] Financially, God wants us to prosper and have all our basic needs met.[36]

Wellness: The Awareness of the Whole Individual

Spiritual Wellness

More importantly, God wants us to know Him intimately, to worship Him, and to spend eternity with Him.[37] We have to be in the right relationship with Him and understand who He is.

He wants us to understand the primary purpose He has given us: to glorify and bring honor to the Lord by drawing closer to Him and bringing others to Him. We often ask ourselves what God's will is for our lives. Some of His purposes for us are very explicitly laid out in His Word—the Bible. Some of His desires for us are less obvious.

One of our young sons once asked if my husband and I thought God would want him to be married or to remain single. Knowing God's plan in this area consumed much of his thoughts and time. We did not know the answer to this question. We counseled him to believe that in that moment, God desired that he be a single man after God's own heart! We used the following analogy: in some instances, knowing God's will is like driving a car at night. You can see only as far as your headlights, and you really *can* make the whole trip that way. You don't always see where you're going, and you don't have to see your final destination or everything you will pass along the way. You just have to see two or three feet ahead of you and move forward into the light of the headlamps.

In our lives, God often only shows us a bit of His will at a time. As we obediently move forward into His revealed will, He shows us more and more. Mark Batterson said, "The plans of God are only revealed in the presence of God. We don't get our marching orders until we get on our knees!"[38]

God wants us to be holy and blessed in every aspect of our lives.[39] A huge portion of Jesus's ministry included healing and restoring people to wholeness.

Wellness: The Awareness of the Whole Individual

He desires that we know Him and make Him known to others. God sets you, the believer, apart so you can share Christ with others through the power of the Lord, who lives and works in and through you.[40] C. Wayne Mayhall said, "He [Christ] provided for people's immediate and physical needs but also prepared them to see their spiritual needs. He delivered the people from the enemy but also directed them to the Father."[41]

How do we live according to God's desires?

- Strive to enjoy a deep and personal relationship with Christ. His presence and His will must become more important than our own.[42] We must die to our selfish nature and cultivate His loving nature. I had a counseling supervisor who would ask her clients (and me), "What do you want? Do you want it badly enough to obey God to have it?" If you're like me, I want to desire God's will most of the time, but if I am honest, my own prevailing hopes influence everything I do and say! Still, I continue to strive to want what God wants.

- Allow the Holy Spirit to work as the motivating force in our life.

- Walk with Jesus—let His presence and peace overflow in our heart. When we are no longer in regular communion with God, immediately take steps to identify any sin in your life, confess it to Christ and others, and enjoy the restoration of our fellowship with Him. Then, continue our walk with Him with His peace filling our heart and mind.

- Do our best to be a person who can be trusted, to be the salt of the earth adding flavor to those we introduce to Christ, and to be the light of the world exposing darkness and enlightening others with knowledge of Christ's forgiveness and love.[43]

Wellness: The Awareness of the Whole Individual

- Pray to stay in contact with Christ, to remain dependent on Him, to grow, and to develop our capacity to love and cherish others in Christ.
- Be "separate." Let God's holiness overflow.[44]
- Study God's Word on a daily basis in order to develop Christian perspectives. Be a worker approved by God![45]
- Fellowship with and show love to other believers. Attend church.[46]

Challenges: Spiritual Wellness Is Not Necessarily about Being Happy

Gary Thomas wrote the book *Sacred Marriage*.[47] I love his subtitle, "What if God designed marriage to make us holy more than to make us happy?" If God wants us to be spiritually whole, we can trust that He will use any means necessary to turn our heads and our hearts toward Him.

Yes, God cares about our happiness and our blessedness, but Thomas points out that these are not the lens through which we gain a perspective on life. Life situations can help us draw our sense of meaning, purpose, and fulfillment from God. They teach us to see and wait on God to transform us into fulfilled beings with a deeper sense of meaning and a fuller understanding of His purpose in our relationships. After all, our trials and struggles are temporary in the light of eternity. God alone can fill the spiritual ache in our souls and make us spiritually whole. Spiritual growth is our goal; our life is His canvas. So, we humanly, imperfectly endeavor to love God more and reflect the character of his Son daily.

Wellness: The Awareness of the Whole Individual

Spiritual Wellness Is Not Necessarily About the Absence of Trials

The Beatitudes

And he opened his mouth and taught them, saying:

"Blessed are the poor in spirit, for theirs is the kingdom of heaven.

"Blessed are those who mourn, for they shall be comforted.

"Blessed are the meek, for they shall inherit the earth.

"Blessed are those who hunger and thirst for righteousness, for they shall be satisfied.

"Blessed are the merciful, for they shall receive mercy.

"Blessed are the pure in heart, for they shall see God.

"Blessed are the peacemakers, for they shall be called sons of God.

"Blessed are those who are persecuted for righteousness' sake, for theirs is the kingdom of heaven.

"Blessed are you when others revile you and persecute you and utter all kinds of evil against you falsely on my account.

Rejoice and be glad, for your reward is great in heaven, for so they persecuted the prophets who were before you.[48]

    The Beatitudes come from the opening verses of the famous Sermon on the Mount delivered by Jesus and recorded in the gospel of Matthew. Here, Jesus states several blessings, each beginning with the phrase, "Blessed are . . ." Each saying speaks of a blessing or "divine favor" bestowed upon a person resulting from the possession of a certain character quality.

    The word "beatitude" comes from the Latin *beatitudo,* meaning "blessedness." The phrase "blessed are" in each of the beatitudes implies a *current* state of well-being. Jesus was saying those who

Wellness: The Awareness of the Whole Individual

possess these inward qualities would be divinely blessed with future rewards, even though we suffer persecutions and endure trials now.

I love the stories of Ezra and Nehemiah and the struggles they endured to rebuild the Temple and to restore and renew God's people spiritually, then to reconstruct the walls of Jerusalem. They were captives—they were considered the enemy—and yet, God turned the heads and hearts of some of the vilest pagan kings to bring about His purposes in rebuilding. He provided huge amounts of money, transportation, supplies, protection, and governance through these evil rulers, and Jerusalem was restored!

God can use the challenges and celebrations of our lives to turn our hearts and heads toward Him as we grow in character. His desire is less to make us happy and more to make us holy—set apart for Him and like Him in all ways. The struggles, suffering, and trials we face are ordained by God with this single purpose!

Is there a purpose for the challenges God brings our way? A former Pastor of mine once explained to us that there were three reasons for suffering in the form of sickness.

- There is a suffering or a sickness unto death. Every living thing will die.[49]

- Sickness unto chastisement[50]—God rebukes and disciplines those He loves.[51] The connection between physical disease and lack of thorough spiritual examination is common. We may experience affliction for specific sins—if I abuse food, drugs, and more, I will suffer physical consequences. If it is a sickness unto chastisement, we need to confess our faults and seek forgiveness from God and those against whom we have sinned.

- Sickness to manifest the work of God and to glorify Him.[52] We may experience trials:

Wellness: The Awareness of the Whole Individual

- to help purify and strengthen our faith for God's glory.[53]
- to develop patience in us to keep God's principles.
- to promote sanctification for our growth in Christ.
- to teach us important lessons.
- to show that His grace will always be sufficient.[54]
- to show that everything works for the good of those who love the Lord and are called according to His purposes.[55]
- to renew our minds. When we are tempted, He will also provide a way out so we can stand up under it.[56]
- to produce perseverance.[57]
- so that our faith may be purified as gold is refined by fire.[58]
- so that we will praise God.[59] Paul and Silas were flogged and imprisoned, and their feet were fastened in stocks, but they still prayed and sang hymns to God for the sake of the gospel!

We need to discern whether we have a sickness unto death, unto chastisement, or unto the glory of God.[60]

Although we suffer in many ways, we do not lose heart and we have hope! God strengthens us day by day, and we look forward to an eternal reward as Paul did in 2 Corinthians 4:8–18. We are to pray a prayer of faith that discerns and visualizes what God intends to do, and then our future prayer is made in harmony with that discernment.

Spiritual Wellness Is about Peace

God will walk us through even the most difficult of journeys to wellness, or "shalom."

Shalom is peace—nothing missing, nothing broken, wholeness, completeness. It is deep and wide and touches every area of our lives. It is the supernatural definition of wellness.

Wellness: The Awareness of the Whole Individual

God's will for us is wellness—to be able to live an abundant, healthy, and prosperous life. Wellness also includes having a healthy relationship with God and discovering who we are in Christ. God's ways will bring us peace beyond understanding, even while we are being challenged with life's situations. Take time to learn of Him and His will as found in His Word.

Spiritual Wellness Assessment

At our counseling and coaching offices, we use the BELIEFS acrostic as a tool to ensure we are helping those who come to us for wise counsel to examine their lives from multiple dimensions off wellness.

Body
Emotions
Livelihood
Intellect
Environment
Family/Friends
Spiritual

If I were to take the BELIEFS acrostic and divide each of the seven dimensions of wellness into pieces of a pie, my pie would include only six pieces of pie and the spiritual dimension would cover this pie like one big piecrust. I believe that the spirit is the most important dimension, and as a Christian, I hope that what I believe about God and my theology covers and influences all other dimensions of my well-being.

How would you draw these seven dimensions of wellness to represent your ideal life? How would you answer the following questions? There is no right or wrong answer—each individual is unique.

Wellness: The Awareness of the Whole Individual

True	False	I am a fully spiritual being, having a human experience!
True	False	God wants me to know Him intimately and to worship Him.[61]
True	False	I will spend eternity with Him because Jesus Christ is my Savior and Lord.[62]
True	False	My chief aim is to glorify and bring honor to the Lord by drawing closer to Him and bringing others to Him.[63]
True	False	God wants me to be holy and blessed in every aspect of my life.[64]
True	False	I strive to make Him known to others.[65]
True	False	I am experiencing wellness and peace ("shalom") on this journey.
Total ____	Total ____	

Wellness: The Awareness of the Whole Individual

Wellness: The Awareness of the Whole Individual

SPIRITUAL WELLNESS ASSESSMENT

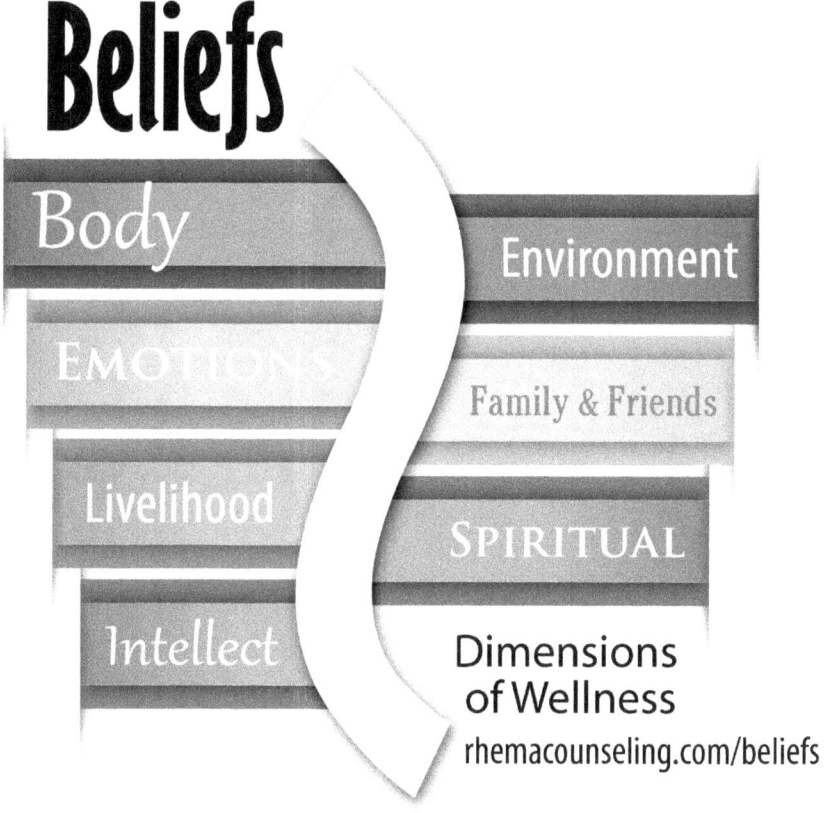

Dimensions of Wellness
rhemacounseling.com/beliefs

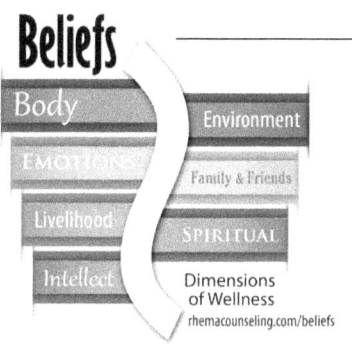

Spiritual Wellness Assessment:
The Awareness of the Whole Individual

At our counseling and coaching offices, we use the BELIEFS acrostic as a tool to ensure we are helping those who come to us for wise counsel to examine their lives from multiple dimensions off wellness.

Body
Emotions
Livelihood
Intellect
Environment
Family/Friends
Spiritual

Begin this self-assessment to see which areas of your life need focus and prayer.

General

True	False	
		I attempt to attend to all 7 dimensions of wellness when making important decisions.

Wellness: The Awareness of the Whole Individual

Body

True	False	I honor God by paying attention to and caring for my physical health.
True	False	I treat my body as a temple of the Holy Spirit that is on loan to me.
True	False	My body belongs to God.
True	False	I exercise at least three times a week.
True	False	I am consciously aware of what I am eating and drinking and what is good for my body.
True	False	When I go grocery shopping, I normally look for nutritious items.
True	False	I want to learn how to honor God in this area of my life.
Total ___	Total ___	

Wellness: The Awareness of the Whole Individual

Emotions

True	False	
True	False	I desire perfect peace – to be steady, calm, and confident in who I am and Who the Lord is.
True	False	Emotions are natural – a part of being made in the image of God.
True	False	The Holy Spirit will interact with my spirit to train me to live as the Lord directs.
True	False	To direct my emotions, I have to direct my thinking according to God's will.
True	False	I strive to bring my perspectives in line with those that honor God.
True	False	I desire to Rejoice in the Lord always!
True	False	I want to learn how to honor God in this area of my life.
Total ___	Total ___	

Wellness: The Awareness of the Whole Individual

Livelihood

True	False	God Himself works: He created the world in an orderly fashion to reflect His good purposes
True	False	As God's image bearers, we are designed to work and play a unique role in the world.
True	False	In our brokenness, we tend to view work in unhealthy ways ignoring God's perspective in our work.
True	False	Only God (not our livelihood or accomplishments) can satisfy our longings and help us find rest for our souls.
True	False	We were created to reflect God's own productive nature, and when we neglect this responsibility, we unfairly put burdens on others.
True	False	While we may not be able to escape challenges in our work, we can still honor God in all we do.
True	False	A godly understanding of work encompasses being good stewards entrusted with talents and attributes.
Total ____	Total ____	

Wellness: The Awareness of the Whole Individual

Intellect

True	False	I have treasured God's word in my heart and I meditate on His precepts. (Psalm 119:9-16)
True	False	I participate in creative and stimulating mental activities regularly.
True	False	I use many available resources to learn about and discover the world around me.
True	False	I remain open to new ideas and experiences.
True	False	I am determined to expand my knowledge and improve my skills for a healthy lifestyle.
True	False	Scripture is clear that the obligation of teaching and training the child belongs to the parent.
True	False	I strive to enhance the intellectual stimulation of my children in many ways.
Total ___	Total ___	

Wellness: The Awareness of the Whole Individual

Environment

True	False	My physical environment is clean and uncluttered.
True	False	I look forward to going home to my living quarters.
True	False	I focus on using positive words with those in my environment.
True	False	I receive positive words from those in my environment.
True	False	My environment is free from any sexual images (music, television, computer, magazines and books).
True	False	I live in and promote an environment that displays Biblical love.
True	False	I am safe and free from physical and sexual abuse.
Total ____	Total ____	

Wellness: The Awareness of the Whole Individual

Family/Friends

True	False	I have family and friends around me.
True	False	It is peaceful and not quarrelsome in my family.
True	False	I have contentment in my relationship with my family members.
True	False	I am a gift to my family members.
True	False	My family members are a gift to me.
True	False	My family members accept me for who I am and love me no matter what.
True	False	My family is a small world created and surrounded by love.
Total ____	Total ____	

Wellness: The Awareness of the Whole Individual

Spiritual

True	False	I am a fully spiritual being, having a human experience!
True	False	God wants me to know Him intimately and to worship Him.[61]
True	False	I will spend eternity with Him because Jesus Christ is my Savior and Lord.[62]
True	False	My chief aim is to glorify and bring honor to the Lord by drawing closer to Him and bringing others to Him.[63]
True	False	God wants me to be holy and blessed in every aspect of my life.[64]
True	False	I strive to make Him known to others.[65]
True	False	I am experiencing wellness and peace ("shalom") on this journey.
Total ____	Total ____	

Wellness: The Awareness of the Whole Individual

Children

True	False	
True	False	I understand my child's body is God's gift, full of potential, and needs to be nourished and cared for.
True	False	I strive for a strong emotional bond with my child to enhance healthy stress regulation and resilience.
True	False	I teach my child to be responsible in line with her current level of development and abilities.
True	False	I endeavor to intellectually stimulate and interact with my child to prepare him for a future of study and productive living.
True	False	I desire to create a safe and welcoming physical and spiritual environment for my child.
True	False	I encourage rewarding, nurturing, and enduring relationships and connections for my child according to God's design.
True	False	God's love is the key! I teach my child that her relationship with God influences all other earthly connections.
Total ____	Total ____	

Wellness: The Awareness of the Whole Individual

(Endnotes)

1. *Barbara Lockhart, Ed.D. and Ron Hager, Ph.D., Brigham Young University, Provo*

2. <http://definitionofwellness.com>

3. Number 7965, <http://biblehub.com/hebrew/7965.htm>

4. You can make copies of this tool here and/or download this helpful tool at <http://rhemacounseling.com/consultation-supervision>

5. <http://www.westminsterconfession.org/the-doctrines-of-grace/the-triune-god.php>

6. MacDonald, George. (1985) *The Curate's Awakening.* Bethany House Publishers.

7. Butler University, 4600 Sunset Avenue, Indianapolis, IN 46208 <http://www.butler.edu/wellness/intellect>. Accessed January 30, 2015.

8. Howard University, 10901 Little Patuxent Parkway, Columbia, Maryland 21044. <http://www.howardcc.edu/students/wellness_center/intellectual.html> Accessed January 23, 2015.

9. *The Holy Bible: King James Version.*, electronic ed. of the 1769 edition of the 1611 Authorized Version. (Bellingham WA: Logos Research Systems, Inc., 1995), Pr 23:7.

10. Miller, C. (2004). *Nursing for Wellness in Older Adults: Theory and Practice.* 4th Edition. Philadelphia: Williams, Lippincott Williams & Wilcott.

11. Ibid.

12. <http://www.activeminds.com/health.html>. Health & Wellness. *Aging Well: Joy . . . or Pain?* By Suz Redfearn, Special to The Washington Post, August 2, 2005.

Wellness: The Awareness of the Whole Individual

[13] Cohen, G.D. (2005) *The Mature Mind: The Positive Power of the Aging Brain.* New York: Basic Books.

[14] Miller (2004).

[15] Charles Reed Kelley *Dreamer to Dream Maker* Inovo Publishing, Feb. 12, 2014, Page 29.

[16] Frances E., M.D. Jensen and Amy Ellis Nutt; The Teenage Brain: *A Neuroscientist's Survival Guide to Raising Adolescents and Young Adults.* Harper Collins Publishing Hardcover, 358 pages.

[17] Noah Webster, American Dictionary of the English Language, New York, S. Converse, 1828.

[18] Noah Webster, Edited by John Gage, Webster's Dictionary, U.S.A., Ottenheimer Publishers, Inc., 1971, p.128.

[19] RSVP America, *RSVP America Training Manual*, First Principles, Inc., 1996, p. 4.

[20] Ibid.

[21] Jacob Abbott, *Ethics*, Ginn & Company, Boston, 1890, p. 78.

[22] RSVP America, *RSVP America Training Manual*, First Principles, Inc., 1996, p. 28.

[23] Judith A. Reisman, Ph.D., Toxic Media Alters the Human Brain, Subverting Free Speech Law & Public Policies, Paper authorized by the Ontario Human Rights Commission, Ontario, Canada, Jan. 1993, p. 23.

[24] Judith A. Reisman, Ph.D., Toxic Media Alters the Human Brain, Subverting Free Speech Law & Public Policies, Paper authorized by the Ontario Human Rights Commission, Ontario, Canada, Jan. 1993, p. 1.

[25] Judith A. Reisman, Ph.D., *Soft Porn Plays Hardball*, Huntington House Publishers, Lafayette, LA, 1991, p.14.

26 Google Violence and Traumatic Stress Research Branch, Division of Applied and Services Research, National Institute of Mental Health for more information on this subject.

27 Go to www.barna.org to obtain these statistics.

28 McGrath, A. E. (1999). *The NIV Thematic Reference Bible.* Zondervan Publishing House. McGrath, A. E. (1999). The NIV Thematic Reference Bible. Zondervan publishing house. Grand Rapids, Michigan.

29 <www.oxforddictionaries.com/us>

30 Nikelly, A. G. (2005). "Positive health outcome of social interest." *Journal of Individual Psychology* 61.4. Nikelly, A. G. (2005). Positive health outcome of social interest. Journal of individual psychology. Vol 61.4. The University of Texas Press, Austin, TX.

31 Minuchin, S. (1974). Families and Family Therapy. Minuchin, S. (1974). Families & family therapy. Harvard university press, Cambridge, Massachusetts.

32 Colapinto, G. (1982). Structural Family Therapy. Colapinto, G. (1982). Structural family therapy. Originally published in Arthur M. Horne and Merle M. Ohlsen (eds.), Family counseling and Therapy. Itasca, Illinois: F .E .Peacock.

33 He "heals all your diseases" (Psalms 103:3, ESV); "…with His wounds we are healed" (Isaiah 53:5, ESV). *See also* Matthew 5:17 and 1 Peter 2:24.

34 "The thief comes only to steal and kill and destroy. I came that they may have life and have it abundantly" (John 10:10, ESV).

35 "But the fruit of the Spirit is love, joy, peace, patience, kindness, goodness, faithfulness, gentleness, self-control; against such things there is no law" (Galatians 5:22–23, ESV); "…casting all your anxieties on Him, because He cares for you" (1 Peter 5:7, ESV).

36 "Beloved, I pray that all may go well with you and that you may be in good health, as it goes well with your soul" (3 John 1:2, ESV); "Let those who delight in My righteousness shout for joy and be glad and say evermore, 'Great is the LORD, who delights in the welfare of His servant!'" (Psalm 35:27, ESV). *See also* Matthew 6:33.

37 "For God so loved the world, that He gave His only Son, that whoever believes in Him should not perish but have eternal life. For God did not send His Son into the world to condemn the world, but in order that the world might be saved through Him" (John 3:16–17, ESV); "And this is eternal life, that they know You, the only true God, and Jesus Christ whom You have sent" (John 17:3, ESV).

38 Batterson, Mark. *Draw the Circle: The 40-day Prayer Challenge.* Grand Rapids, MI: Zondervan, 2012. Print.

39 *See* Mark 10:52.

40 "...He who has set me apart before I was born, and who called me by His grace, was pleased to reveal His Son to me, in order that I might preach Him among the Gentiles" (Galatians 1:15–16, ESV); "It is no longer I who live, but Christ who lives in me. And the life I now live in the flesh I live by faith in the Son of God, who loved me, and gave Himself for me" (Galatians 2:20, ESV).

41 Mayhall, C. Wayne. "To Know Christ and to Make Him Known." Christian Research Institute, 11 June 2009. Web. 27 May 2015. <http://www.equip.org/article/to-know-christ-and-to-make-him-known>.

42 "It is no longer I who live, but Christ who lives in me" (Galatians 2:20, ESV).

43 *See* Matthew 5:13–14.

44 "As He who called you is holy, you also be holy in all your conduct, since it is written, 'You shall be holy, for I am holy'" (1 Peter 1:15–16, ESV).

[45] "Do your best to present [study to show] yourself to God as one approved, a worker who has no need to be ashamed, rightly handling the word of truth" (2 Timothy 2:15); "And they devoted themselves to the apostles' teaching and fellowship, to the breaking of bread and the prayers . . ." (Acts 2:42, ESV).

[46] "And let us consider how to stir up one another to love and good works, not neglecting to meet together, as is the habit of some, but encouraging one another, and all the more as you see the Day drawing near" (Hebrews 10:24–25, ESV); "Whoever says he is in the light and hates his brother is still in darkness. Whoever loves his brother abides in the light" 1 John 2:9–10, ESV).

[47] Thomas, Gary. *Sacred Marriage: What If God Designed Marriage to Make Us Holy More than to Make Us Happy?* Grand Rapids, MI: Zondervan Pub. House, 2000. Print.

[48] Matthew 5:3–12 (ESV).

[49] "For everything there is a season, and a time for every matter under heaven: a time to be born, and a time to die . . ." (Ecclesiastes 3:1–2, ESV); "The years of our life are seventy, or even by reason of strength eighty; yet their span is but toil and trouble; they are soon gone, and we fly away" (Psalm 90:10, ESV).

[50] *See* 1 Corinthians 11:28–33.

[51] *See* Revelation 3:14–22.

[52] *See* 2 Corinthians 12:6; John 9:2, 3.

[53] *See* 1 Peter 1:6–7; John 9:1–3.

[54] *See* 2 Corinthians 12:7–10.

[55] *See* Romans 8:28.

[56] *See* 1 Corinthians 10:13.

Wellness: The Awareness of the Whole Individual

57 *See* James 1:2–4.

58 *See* 1 Peter 1:7–8.

59 *See* Psalms 27:5–6; & 16:16–28.

60 *See* James 5:14–16; 1 Corinthians 11:27–32; John 11:4.

61 *See* John 3:16.

62 *See* John 17:3.

63 *See* Colossians 3:17.

64 *See* Mark 10:52.

65 *See* Galatians 1:15.

66 *See* John 3:16.

67 *See* John 17:3.

68 *See* Colossians 3:17.

69 *See* Mark 10:52.

70 *See* Galatians 1:15.

www.ingramcontent.com/pod-product-compliance
Lightning Source LLC
Chambersburg PA
CBHW071521080526
44588CB00011B/1513